Mediterranean
COOKING

Publications International, Ltd.
Favorite Brand Name Recipes at www.fbnr.com

Pictured on the front cover: Mediterranean Stew *(page 178)*.

Pictured on the back cover *(top to bottom):* Shrimp Scampi *(page 80)* and Spanish Paella-Style Rice *(page 180)*.

Illustrated by Roberta Polfus.

ISBN-13: 978-1-4127-2579-8
ISBN-10: 1-4127-2579-8

Library of Congress Control Number: 2007921114

Manufactured in China.

8 7 6 5 4 3 2 1

Microwave Cooking: Microwave ovens vary in wattage. Use the cooking times as guidelines and check for doneness before adding more time.

Preparation/Cooking Times: Preparation times are based on the approximate amount of time required to assemble the recipe before cooking, baking, chilling or serving. These times include preparation steps such as measuring, chopping and mixing. The fact that some preparations and cooking can be done simultaneously is taken into account. Preparation of optional ingredients and serving suggestions is not included.

Table of Contents

Small Plates

Roasted Eggplant Dip
Makes 8 servings

2 eggplants (about 1 pound each)
¼ cup lemon juice
3 tablespoons sesame tahini*
4 cloves garlic, minced
2 teaspoons hot pepper sauce
½ teaspoon salt
   Pita bread rounds, cut into wedges
   Paprika
1 tablespoon chopped fresh parsley
   Red chile pepper slices**

*Available in the ethnic section of the supermarket or in Middle Eastern grocery stores.

**Chile peppers can sting and irritate the skin, so wear rubber gloves when handling peppers and do not touch your eyes.

1. Prepare grill for direct cooking. Prick eggplants in several places with fork. Place eggplants on grid. Grill, covered, over medium-high heat 30 to 40 minutes or until skin is black and blistered and pulp is soft, turning often. Peel eggplants when cool enough to handle. Let cool to room temperature.

2. Place eggplant pulp in food processor with lemon juice, tahini, garlic, pepper sauce and salt; process until smooth. Refrigerate at least 1 hour before serving to allow flavors to blend. Serve with pita. Garnish with paprika, parsley and red pepper slices.

Shrimp Tapas in Sherry Sauce

Makes 4 appetizer servings

1 slice thick-cut bacon, cut into ¼-inch strips
2 tablespoons olive oil
2 ounces crimini or button mushrooms, sliced into quarters
½ pound large raw shrimp (about 16 shrimp), peeled and deveined,
    leaving tails attached
2 cloves garlic, thinly sliced
2 tablespoons medium dry sherry
1 tablespoon fresh lemon juice
¼ teaspoon red pepper flakes

1. Cook bacon in large skillet over medium heat until brown and crispy.
Remove from skillet with slotted spoon; drain on paper towels. Set
aside.

2. Add oil to bacon drippings in skillet. Add mushrooms; cook and
stir 2 minutes. Add shrimp and garlic; cook and stir 3 minutes or until
shrimp turn pink and opaque. Stir in sherry, lemon juice and red pepper
flakes.

3. Remove shrimp to serving bowl with slotted spoon. Cook sauce
1 minute or until reduced and thickened. Pour over shrimp. Sprinkle
with reserved bacon.

*Note: Tapas are Spanish appetizers, tidbits of food
for nibbling with drinks. These dishes range
from something as simple as a bowl of olives
to more elaborate preparations such as cold
potato omelets and shrimp cooked in sherry
sauce. Tapas are generally accompanied by
sherry or other cocktails.*

Shrimp Tapas in Sherry Sauce

7

Arborio Rice Pilaf Croquettes

Makes 4 to 6 servings

      White Sauce (page 10)
    1 tablespoon butter
    1 tablespoon olive oil
    1 small onion, chopped
    1 cup uncooked arborio rice
    1 clove garlic, minced
    3 tablespoons dry white wine
  2¼ cups chicken broth
    ½ teaspoon salt
    3 tablespoons pine nuts, toasted
    2 tablespoons golden raisins
    2 tablespoons chopped fresh basil
    ¼ teaspoon black pepper
    3 cups Italian-seasoned bread crumbs
    3 eggs, lightly beaten
    2 tablespoons cold water
    ½ cup vegetable oil

1. Prepare White Sauce; set aside.

2. Heat butter and olive oil in large saucepan over medium heat until butter melts. Add onion; cook and stir about 3 minutes or until tender. Add rice and garlic; stir until rice is coated. Add wine; stir until liquid is absorbed.

3. Stir in chicken broth and salt. Bring to a boil over medium-high heat. Reduce heat to low; simmer, covered, 20 minutes or until rice is tender and liquid is absorbed. Remove from heat. Cover; let stand 5 minutes.

continued on page 10

Arborio Rice Pilaf Croquettes

Arborio Rice Pilaf Croquettes, continued

4. Transfer mixture to large bowl. Stir in White Sauce, pine nuts, raisins, basil and pepper. To form croquette, scoop out rice mixture using ¼-cup measure. Shape rice mixture into ball, flatten slightly. Place croquette on waxed paper-lined baking sheet. Repeat with remaining rice mixture. Cover; refrigerate 1 hour.

5. Spread bread crumbs in shallow bowl. Whisk together eggs and water in separate shallow bowl. Roll croquette in bread crumbs, then in egg mixture, then in bread crumbs again. Return to waxed paper-lined baking sheet. Repeat with remaining croquettes. Cover and refrigerate.

6. Heat vegetable oil in large, deep skillet. Carefully place 6 croquettes into oil. Cook croquettes about 45 seconds on each side or until golden brown. Remove to paper towels with slotted spoon. Repeat with remaining croquettes.

White Sauce
Makes about ½ cup sauce

4½ teaspoons butter
4½ teaspoons all-purpose flour
¼ teaspoon salt
½ cup milk, warmed
4½ teaspoons grated Romano cheese
Dash ground nutmeg

1. Melt butter in 1-quart saucepan over medium heat. Add flour and salt; stir to blend. Add milk; stir to blend. Bring to a boil over high heat, stirring constantly. Reduce heat to low; simmer, uncovered, 2 to 3 minutes until slightly thickened.

2. Remove from heat. Stir in cheese and nutmeg.

Spanish Potato Omelet

Makes 8 servings

¼ cup olive oil
¼ cup vegetable oil
1 pound unpeeled red or white potatoes, cut into ⅛-inch slices
½ teaspoon salt, divided
1 small onion, cut in half lengthwise, thinly sliced crosswise
¼ cup chopped green bell pepper
¼ cup chopped red bell pepper
3 eggs

1. Heat oils in large skillet over medium-high heat. Add potatoes to hot oil. Turn with spatula several times to coat all slices with oil. Sprinkle with ¼ teaspoon of the salt. Cook 6 to 9 minutes or until potatoes become translucent, turning occasionally. Add onion and peppers. Reduce heat to medium. Cook 10 minutes or until potatoes are tender, turning occasionally. Drain mixture in colander placed in large bowl; reserve oil. Let potato mixture stand until cool. Beat eggs with remaining ¼ teaspoon salt in large bowl. Gently stir in potato mixture; lightly press into bowl until mixture is covered with eggs. Let stand 15 minutes.

2. Heat 2 teaspoons reserved oil in 6-inch nonstick skillet over medium-high heat. Spread potato mixture in pan to form solid layer. Cook until egg on bottom and side of pan has set but top still looks moist. Cover pan with plate. Flip omelet onto plate, then slide omelet back into pan. Continue to cook until bottom is lightly browned. Slide omelet onto serving plate. Let stand 30 minutes before serving. Cut into wedges.

Note: In Spain, an omelet made with eggs and potatoes is called a tortilla. The classic tortilla is large and thick—almost solid with potatoes. It is served at room temperature any time of day.

Small Plates

Olive Tapenade Dip

Makes 4 (¼-cup) servings

1½ cups (10-ounce jar) pitted kalamata olives, drained
3 tablespoons olive oil
3 tablespoons *French's®* Spicy Brown Mustard
1 tablespoon minced fresh rosemary leaves
   or 1 teaspoon dried rosemary leaves
1 teaspoon minced garlic

Place all ingredients in food processor. Process until puréed. Serve with vegetable crudités or pita chips.

Spanish Potatoes with Garlic Mayonnaise

Makes 10 to 12 servings

2 pounds red potatoes, cut into 1-inch pieces
2 tablespoons olive oil
1 teaspoon coarse or kosher salt
¾ teaspoon red pepper flakes
1 teaspoon paprika
1 cup mayonnaise
2 cloves garlic, minced

1. Preheat oven to 425°F.

2. Combine potatoes, oil and salt in large bowl; toss to coat. Spread mixture on large baking sheet. Roast 15 minutes. Turn potatoes; sprinkle with pepper flakes. Roast 15 to 20 minutes more or until crisp and brown. Sprinkle with paprika.

3. Meanwhile, combine mayonnaise and garlic in small bowl; blend well. Serve as dipping sauce for potatoes.

Olive Tapenade Dip

Mediterranean Frittata

Makes 6 to 8 appetizer servings

¼ cup olive oil
5 small onions, thinly sliced
1 can (about 14 ounces) whole peeled tomatoes, drained and chopped
¼ pound prosciutto or cooked ham, chopped
¼ cup grated Parmesan cheese
2 tablespoons chopped fresh parsley
½ teaspoon dried marjoram
¼ teaspoon dried basil
¼ teaspoon salt
   Generous dash black pepper
6 eggs
2 tablespoons butter
   Fresh Italian parsley (optional)

1. Heat oil in large skillet over medium-high heat. Add onions; cook and stir 6 to 8 minutes until soft and golden. Reduce heat to medium. Add tomatoes; cook 5 minutes. Remove tomatoes and onions to large bowl with slotted spoon; discard drippings. Cool tomato mixture to room temperature.

2. Stir prosciutto, cheese, parsley, marjoram, basil, salt and pepper into cooled tomato mixture. Whisk eggs in small bowl; stir into prosciutto mixture.

3. Preheat broiler. Heat butter in large broilerproof skillet over medium heat until melted and bubbly; reduce heat to low. Add egg mixture to skillet, spreading evenly. Cook 8 to 10 minutes until all but top ¼ inch of egg mixture is set; shake pan gently to test. *Do not stir.*

4. Place pan under broiler about 4 inches from heat. Broil 1 to 2 minutes until top of egg mixture is set. (Do not brown or frittata will be dry.) Serve hot or at room temperature. Cut into wedges. Garnish with parsley.

Mediterranean Frittata

Chicken Empanada Pie

Makes 8 to 12 servings

2 tablespoons plus 2 teaspoons olive oil
1 cup chopped onion
2 cloves garlic, minced
1 tablespoon paprika
¾ teaspoon ground ginger
½ teaspoon ground cumin
¼ teaspoon ground cinnamon
⅛ teaspoon ground red pepper
3 cups shredded cooked chicken
¼ teaspoon salt
1 can (about 14 ounces) diced tomatoes
⅓ cup raisins
¼ cup sliced pimiento-stuffed green olives
1 package (about 17 ounces) frozen puff pastry, thawed
½ cup slivered almonds or pine nuts, toasted
   Powdered sugar (optional)

1. Heat 2 tablespoons oil in large skillet over medium heat. Add onions and garlic; cook and stir 5 to 8 minutes or until lightly browned. Stir in paprika, ginger, cumin, cinnamon and red pepper. Add chicken, tomatoes, raisins and olives; cook 8 to 10 minutes. Cool completely.*

2. Preheat oven to 400°F. Brush 17×11-inch baking pan with remaining 2 teaspoons oil.

3. Roll out 1 pastry sheet on lightly floured surface into 14×10-inch rectangle. Place on prepared pan. Spread filling evenly over pastry to within 1 inch of edge. Sprinkle almonds over filling. Moisten edges with water. Roll out remaining pastry sheet to slightly smaller rectangle. Place over filling. Cut 4 slits in top of pastry. Fold edges of bottom pastry over top; press edges together to seal.

4. Bake 30 to 35 minutes or until golden brown. Cool. Dust with powdered sugar.

Filling can be prepared ahead of time.

Hummus Vegetable Dip

Makes about 1¼ cups dip

1 (16-ounce) can chick-peas, rinsed and well drained
5 tablespoons lemon juice
¼ cup water
¼ cup tahini (sesame seed paste)
2 tablespoons FILIPPO BERIO® Olive Oil
1 to 2 cloves garlic, sliced
¼ teaspoon ground cumin
   Salt and freshly ground black pepper
   Few drops hot pepper sauce (optional)
   Additional lemon juice (optional)
   Assorted cut-up fresh vegetables
   Pita bread wedges
   Oil-cured black olives (optional)
   Additional FILIPPO BERIO® Olive Oil (optional)

In blender container or food processor, place chick-peas, 5 tablespoons lemon juice, water, tahini, 2 tablespoons olive oil, garlic and cumin; process until mixture is thick and creamy. Season to taste with salt, black pepper and hot pepper sauce, if desired. Adjust consistency with additional lemon juice or water, if desired. Transfer to serving bowl. Cover; refrigerate at least 1 hour before serving. Serve with vegetables and pita bread; garnish dip with olives and drizzle of additional olive oil, if desired.

Small Plates

Spanish-Style Garlic Shrimp
Makes 6 servings

4 tablespoons I CAN'T BELIEVE IT'S NOT BUTTER!® Spread, divided
1 pound uncooked medium shrimp, peeled and deveined
½ teaspoon salt
2 cloves garlic, finely chopped
½ to 1 jalapeño pepper, seeded and finely chopped
¼ cup chopped fresh cilantro or parsley
1 tablespoon fresh lime juice

In 12-inch nonstick skillet, melt 1 tablespoon I Can't Believe It's Not Butter!® Spread over high heat and cook shrimp with salt 2 minutes or until shrimp are almost pink, turning once. Remove shrimp and set aside.

In same skillet, melt remaining 3 tablespoons I Can't Believe It's Not Butter!® Spread over medium-low heat and cook garlic and jalapeño pepper, stirring occasionally, 1 minute. Return shrimp to skillet. Stir in cilantro and lime juice and heat 30 seconds or until shrimp turn pink. Serve, if desired, with crusty Italian bread.

Note: Many variations of shrimp are served as tapas in every region of Spain. They are usually served in "cazuelas"—small earthenware casserole-like dishes that come in all shapes and sizes. Cazuelas retain heat and are usually ovenproof, which make them perfect for keeping tapas dishes hot.

Spanish-Style Garlic Shrimp

Roasted Eggplant Spread

Makes 4 servings

1 large eggplant
1 can (about 14 ounces) diced tomatoes, drained
½ cup finely chopped green onions
½ cup chopped fresh parsley
2 tablespoons red wine vinegar
1 tablespoon olive oil
3 cloves garlic, finely chopped
½ teaspoon salt
½ teaspoon dried oregano
2 (8-inch) rounds pita bread
　Fresh lemon or lime wedges (optional)

1. Preheat oven to 375°F.

2. Place eggplant on baking sheet. Bake 1 hour or until tender, turning occasionally. Remove eggplant from oven. Let stand 10 minutes or until cool enough to handle.

3. Cut eggplant in half lengthwise; remove pulp. Discard stem and skin. Place pulp in medium bowl; mash with fork until smooth. Add tomatoes, green onions, parsley, vinegar, oil, garlic, salt and oregano; blend well. Cover eggplant mixture; refrigerate 2 hours.

4. Preheat broiler. Split pitas horizontally in half to form 4 rounds. Stack pita rounds; cut into sixths to form 24 wedges. Place wedges on baking sheet. Broil 4 inches from heat 3 minutes or until crisp.

5. Serve eggplant spread with warm pita wedges. Garnish with lemon.

Roasted Eggplant Spread

Small Plates

Lamb Meatballs
with Tomato Mint Dip

Makes 10 dozen meatballs

1½ cups fine bulgur wheat
 3 cups cold water
 2 pounds ground American lamb
 1 cup minced fresh parsley
 2 medium onions, minced
 1 tablespoon salt
 ½ teaspoon ground allspice
 ½ teaspoon ground cinnamon
 ½ teaspoon ground nutmeg
 ½ teaspoon black pepper
 ¼ to ½ teaspoon ground red pepper (to taste)
 1 piece fresh ginger, about 2×1-inch, peeled and minced
 1 cup ice water
   Tomato Mint Dip (page 23)

Place bulgur in medium bowl: add water. Let soak about 10 minutes. Drain and place in fine meshed strainer; squeeze out water.

In large bowl, knead lamb with parsley, onions, seasonings and ginger. Add bulgur; knead well. Add enough ice water to keep mixture smooth. Use about 1 teaspoon meat mixture to make bite-sized meatballs. Place on ungreased jelly-roll pan. Bake in preheated 375°F oven 20 minutes. Meanwhile, prepare Tomato Mint Dip.

Place meatballs in serving bowl; keep warm. Serve hot with dip.

Favorite recipe from **American Lamb Council**

Tomato Mint Dip

    2 cans (15 ounces each) tomato sauce with tomato bits
1½ teaspoons ground allspice
    1 teaspoon dried mint

In small saucepan, heat all ingredients about 5 minutes to blend flavors.

Favorite recipe from **American Lamb Council**

Caponata

Makes approximately 4½ cups

    1 pound eggplant, cut into ½-inch cubes
    3 large cloves garlic, minced
¼ cup olive oil
    1 can (14½ ounces) **DEL MONTE®** Diced Tomatoes with
        Basil, Garlic & Oregano
    1 medium green pepper, finely chopped
    1 can (2¼ ounces) chopped ripe olives, drained
    2 tablespoons lemon juice
    1 teaspoon dried basil, crushed
    1 baguette French bread, cut into ¼-inch slices

1. Cook eggplant and garlic in oil in large skillet over medium heat
5 minutes. Season with salt and pepper, if desired.

2. Stir in remaining ingredients except bread. Cook, uncovered,
10 minutes or until thickened.

3. Cover and chill. Serve with bread.

Prep Time: 10 minutes • ***Cook Time:*** 15 minutes • ***Chill Time:*** 2 hours

Antipasto
with Marinated Mushrooms

Makes 6 to 8 servings

Marinated Mushrooms (page 25)
4 teaspoons red wine vinegar
½ teaspoon dried basil
½ teaspoon dried oregano
Generous dash black pepper
¼ cup extra-virgin olive oil
4 ounces mozzarella cheese, cut into ½-inch cubes
4 ounces prosciutto or cooked ham, thinly sliced
4 ounces provolone cheese, cut into 2-inch sticks
1 jar (10 ounces) peperoncini peppers, drained
8 ounces hard salami, thinly sliced
2 jars (6 ounces each) marinated artichoke hearts, drained
1 can (6 ounces) pitted black olives, drained
Fresh basil leaves or chives (optional)

1. Prepare Marinated Mushrooms; set aside. Combine vinegar, dried basil, oregano and black pepper in small bowl. Add oil; whisk until well blended. Add mozzarella cubes; stir to coat. Marinate, covered, in refrigerator at least 2 hours.

2. Drain mozzarella cubes, reserving marinade. Wrap 1 prosciutto slice around each provolone stick; roll up remaining slices separately. Arrange mozzarella cubes, prosciutto-wrapped provolone sticks, prosciutto rolls, Marinated Mushrooms, peperoncini, salami, artichoke hearts and olives on large platter.

3. Drizzle reserved marinade over peperoncini, artichoke hearts and olives. Garnish with fresh basil. Serve with small forks or toothpicks.

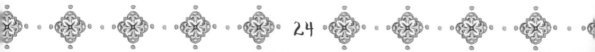

Marinated Mushrooms

  3 tablespoons lemon juice
  2 tablespoons chopped fresh parsley
  1 clove garlic, crushed
½ teaspoon salt
¼ teaspoon dried tarragon
⅛ teaspoon black pepper
½ cup extra-virgin olive oil
½ pound small or medium fresh mushrooms, stems removed

Combine lemon juice, parsley, garlic, salt, tarragon and pepper in medium bowl. Add oil; whisk until well blended. Add mushrooms; stir to coat. Marinate, covered, in refrigerator 4 hours or overnight, stirring occasionally. Drain mushrooms; reserve marinade for dressing.

Antipasto with Marinated Mushrooms

Small Plates

Tomato and Caper Crostini
Makes 2 servings

    1 French roll, cut into 8 slices
    2 plum tomatoes, finely chopped (about 4 ounces)
 1½ tablespoons capers
 1½ teaspoons dried basil
    1 teaspoon extra-virgin olive oil
    1 ounce crumbled feta cheese with sun-dried tomatoes and basil, or any variety

1. Preheat oven to 350°F. Place bread slices on ungreased baking sheet in single layer. Bake 15 minutes or just until golden brown. Cool completely.

2. Meanwhile, combine tomatoes, capers, basil and oil in small bowl; mix well. Just before serving, spoon tomato mixture on each bread slice; sprinkle with cheese.

Sangria
Makes about 6 (8-ounce) servings

    1 cup KARO® Light Corn Syrup
    2 lemons, sliced
    1 orange, sliced
 ½ cup brandy
    1 bottle (750 ml) dry red wine
    2 tablespoons lemon juice
    1 bottle (12 ounces) club soda or seltzer, chilled

1. In large pitcher combine corn syrup, lemon and orange slices and brandy. Let stand 20 to 30 minutes, stirring occasionally. Stir in wine and lemon juice. Refrigerate.

2. Just before serving, add soda and ice cubes.

Tomato and Caper Crostini

Small Plates

Mediterranean Sausage and Spinach Tartlets

Makes 30 appetizers

1 (16-ounce) package PERDUE® Fresh Seasoned Lean Turkey Sausage, Sweet Italian
½ cup frozen chopped spinach, thawed and squeezed dry
1 cup crumbled feta cheese
2 green onions, minced
1½ teaspoons chopped fresh oregano
Salt and pepper, to taste
2 (2.1-ounce) packages mini fillo dough shells
15 pitted kalamata olives, halved

Preheat oven to 375°F.

Remove sausage from casing and place in a large, nonstick skillet over high heat. Sauté until cooked through, breaking up sausage with a wooden spoon as it cooks. Stir in spinach until hot. Turn off heat, stir in feta, green onions, oregano, and salt and pepper to taste.

Set fillo cups on a baking sheet and bake them until crisp and hot, about 4 minutes. Fill each cup with sausage mixture and top with an olive half. Serve immediately.

Note: Whether grilled or added as a flavoring ingredient to sauces, soups or stews, sausages are a key ingredient in many Mediterranean dishes. The most commonly known Spanish and Portuguese sausages are Chorizo (or chouriço) and liquiça. Whether mild or spicy, countless varieties of speciality sausages add great flavor to many dishes.

Taramasalata Vegetable Dip

Makes about 1 cup dip

1 cup (½-inch) fresh bread cubes, crusts removed
4 ounces tarama* (fish roe)
1 small onion, cut into wedges
1 clove garlic, sliced (optional)
½ cup FILIPPO BERIO® Extra Virgin Olive Oil
    Juice of 2 lemons
    Freshly ground black pepper
    Assorted cut-up fresh vegetables
    Lemon wedges (optional)

Fish roe can be found in Middle Eastern or gourmet food shops.

Soak bread cubes in water; press out excess. In blender container or food processor, place tarama; add bread, onion and garlic, if desired. While machine is running, alternately add small amounts of olive oil and lemon juice until mixture is thick and creamy. Transfer to serving bowl. Cover; refrigerate at least 1 hour before serving. Season to taste with pepper. Serve with vegetables; garnish dip with lemon wedges, if desired.

Small Plates

Spanish Tapas Potatoes (Patatas Bravas)

Makes 10 to 12 appetizer servings

Roasted Potatoes
  2½ pounds small red potatoes, quartered
    2 tablespoons olive oil
    1 teaspoon coarse or kosher salt
    ½ teaspoon crushed dried rosemary

Brava Sauce
    1 can (about 14 ounces) diced tomatoes, drained
    ⅓ cup olive oil
    2 tablespoons red wine vinegar
    1 tablespoon minced garlic
    1 tablespoon chili powder
    1 tablespoon paprika
    ¼ teaspoon salt
    ¼ teaspoon chipotle pepper seasoning
    ⅛ to ¼ teaspoon ground red pepper

1. For potatoes, preheat oven to 425°F.

2. Combine potatoes, 2 tablespoons oil, salt and rosemary in large bowl; toss to coat. Spread mixture on large baking sheet. Roast potatoes 35 to 40 minutes or until crisp and brown, turning every 10 minutes.

3 . For sauce, combine tomatoes, ⅓ cup olive oil, vinegar, garlic, chili powder, paprika, salt, chipotle pepper seasoning and red pepper in blender. Process just until blended. Transfer to large saucepan. Cover; cook 5 minutes over medium-high heat until slightly thickened. Cool at room temperature; set aside.

4. To serve, drizzle sauce over potatoes or serve in bowl for dipping.

Note: Sauce can be made up to 24 hours ahead of time. Cover and refrigerate. Bring to room temperature or reheat before serving.

Spanish Tapas Potatoes (Patatas Bravas)

Mediterranean Pita Pizzas

Makes 8 servings

2 (8-inch) rounds pita bread
1 teaspoon olive oil
1 cup canned cannellini beans, rinsed and drained
2 teaspoons lemon juice
2 cloves garlic, minced
½ cup thinly sliced radicchio or escarole lettuce (optional)
½ cup chopped seeded tomato
½ cup finely chopped red onion
¼ cup (1 ounce) crumbled feta cheese
2 tablespoons sliced pitted black olives

1. Preheat oven to 450°F. Arrange pitas on baking sheet; brush tops with oil. Bake 6 minutes.

2. Meanwhile, place beans in small bowl; mash lightly with fork. Stir in lemon juice and garlic. Spread bean mixture evenly onto pitas to within ½ inch of edges. Arrange remaining ingredients on pitas. Bake 5 minutes or until toppings are thoroughly heated and crust is crisp. Cut into wedges; serve hot.

Note: *Pita, also known as pocket bread, is a round, flat Middle Eastern bread. It is usually about six to seven inches in diameter. The bread can be used for a variety of dishes. For a pizza, top warmed rounds with your favorite toppings. For a sandwich, split in half horizontally, open to form a pocket and fill with your favorite sandwich ingredients. Or, cut into wedges, toast and use as dippers for hummus or tapenade.*

Mediterranean Pita Pizzas

Small Plates

Artichoke Frittata

Makes 12 to 16 appetizer servings

1 can (14 ounces) artichoke hearts, drained
3 teaspoons olive oil, divided
½ cup minced green onions
5 eggs
½ cup (2 ounces) shredded Swiss cheese
2 tablespoons grated Parmesan cheese
1 tablespoon minced fresh parsley
1 teaspoon salt
¼ teaspoon black pepper

1. Chop artichoke hearts; set aside.

2. Heat 2 teaspoons oil in 10-inch skillet over medium heat. Add green onions; cook and stir until tender. Remove from skillet.

3. Beat eggs in medium bowl until light. Stir in artichokes, green onions, cheeses, parsley, salt and pepper.

4. Heat remaining 1 teaspoon oil in same skillet over medium heat. Pour egg mixture into skillet. Cook 4 to 5 minutes or until bottom is lightly browned. Place large plate over skillet; invert frittata onto plate. Return frittata, uncooked side down, to skillet. Cook about 4 minutes more or until center is just set. Cut into wedges.

Note: A frittata is an Italian omelet with the ingredients mixed into the eggs. A frittata is firmer than a regular omelet and can be served at room temperature like a Spanish omelet or tortilla.

Olive & Feta Dip

Makes 2 cups dip

1 cup HELLMANN'S® or BEST FOODS® Real Mayonnaise
4 ounces cream cheese, softened
3 ounces feta cheese, crumbled
⅓ cup chopped kalamata olives
3 green onions, chopped
1 clove garlic, pressed or finely chopped
¼ teaspoon dried oregano leaves, crushed

1. Preheat oven to 350°F.

2. In medium bowl combine all ingredients. Spoon into 1½-quart casserole.

3. Bake 30 minutes or until heated through. Serve with pita wedges or your favorite dippers.

Prep Time: 10 Minutes • ***Cook Time:*** 30 Minutes

Grilled Lobster, Shrimp and Calamari Seviche

Makes 6 appetizer servings

¾ cup fresh orange juice
⅓ cup fresh lime juice
2 tablespoons tequila
2 jalapeño peppers,* seeded and minced
2 tablespoons chopped fresh cilantro, chives or green onion tops
1 teaspoon honey
1 teaspoon ground cumin
1 teaspoon olive oil
10 squid, cleaned and cut into rings and tentacles
½ pound medium raw shrimp, peeled, deveined and tails removed
2 lobster tails (8 ounces each), meat removed and shells discarded

Jalapeño peppers can sting and irritate the skin, so wear rubber gloves when handling peppers and do not touch your eyes.

1. For marinade, combine orange juice, lime juice, tequila, jalapeños, cilantro and honey in medium glass bowl.

2. Measure ¼ cup marinade into small glass bowl; stir in cumin and oil. Set aside. Refrigerate remaining marinade.

3. Prepare grill for direct grilling.

4. Bring 1 quart water to a boil in large saucepan over high heat. Add squid; cook 30 seconds or until opaque. Drain. Rinse under cold water; drain. Add squid to refrigerated marinade.

5. Thread shrimp onto metal skewers. Brush shrimp and lobster with reserved ¼ cup marinade.

6. Place lobster on grid. Grill on uncovered grill over medium-hot coals 5 minutes per side or until meat turns opaque and is cooked through. Slice lobster meat into ¼-inch-thick slices; add to squid mixture. Place shrimp on grid. Grill 2 to 3 minutes per side or until shrimp turn pink and opaque. Remove shrimp from skewers; add to squid and lobster mixture.

7. Refrigerate at least 2 hours or overnight.

Grilled Lobster, Shrimp and Calamari Seviche

Small Plates

Herbed Croutons
with Savory Bruschetta

Makes 6 appetizer servings

½ cup regular or reduced fat mayonnaise
¼ cup *French's*® Honey Dijon Mustard
1 tablespoon finely chopped green onion
1 clove garlic, minced
¾ teaspoon dried oregano leaves
1 long thin loaf (18 inches) French bread, cut crosswise
    into ½-inch-thick slices
Savory Bruschetta (recipe follows)

Combine mayonnaise, mustard, onion, garlic and oregano in small bowl; mix well. Spread herbed mixture on one side of each slice of bread.

Place bread, spread sides up, on grid. Grill over medium-low coals 1 minute or until lightly toasted. Spoon Savory Bruschetta onto herbed croutons. Serve warm.

Savory Bruschetta

Makes 3 cups

1 pound ripe plum tomatoes, cored, seeded and chopped
1 cup finely chopped fennel bulb or celery
¼ cup chopped fresh basil leaves
3 tablespoons *French's*® Honey Dijon Mustard
3 tablespoons olive oil
3 tablespoons balsamic vinegar
2 cloves garlic, minced
½ teaspoon salt

Combine ingredients in medium bowl; toss well to coat evenly.

Herbed Croutons with Savory Bruschetta

Tuna Tapenade

Makes 12 servings

1 (7-ounce) STARKIST Flavor Fresh Pouch® Tuna (Albacore
    or Chunk Light)
1 can (6 ounces) pitted ripe olives, drained
4 to 6 anchovy fillets, drained
¼ cup drained capers
2 tablespoons lemon juice
1 tablespoon Dijon-style mustard
1 teaspoon dried basil
2 cloves garlic
⅛ teaspoon ground black pepper
⅓ cup extra-virgin olive oil
    Raw vegetables, crisp wheat crackers or pita bread

In food processor bowl with metal blade, place tuna, olives, anchovies, capers, lemon juice, mustard, basil, garlic and pepper. Add oil very slowly through feed tube while processing. Chill several hours before serving with vegetables.

Prep Time: 7 minutes

Note: A tapenade is a flavorful condiment from southern France. Traditionally, it is made from ground black niçoise olives, anchovies, garlic, capers and olive oil. It is used as a spread for crusty bread or as a dip for raw vegetables. Tapenade is such a popular appetizer that many tasty variations are made today with additional ingredients such as tuna, green olives and mushrooms.

Marinated Antipasto

Makes about 5 cups (12 appetizer servings)

¼ cup extra-virgin olive oil
2 tablespoons balsamic vinegar
1 clove garlic, minced
½ teaspoon sugar
½ teaspoon salt
¼ teaspoon black pepper
1 pint (2 cups) cherry tomatoes
1 can (14 ounces) quartered artichoke hearts, drained
8 ounces small balls or cubes fresh mozzarella cheese
1 cup drained whole pitted kalamata olives
¼ cup julienned or chopped fresh basil

1. Whisk together oil, vinegar, garlic, sugar, salt and pepper in medium bowl. Add tomatoes, artichokes, mozzarella, olives and basil; toss to coat.

2. Let stand at least 30 minutes or cover and chill up to 4 hours (let stand 15 to 30 minutes before serving). Serve at room temperature.

Serving Suggestion: Serve antipasto with toothpicks as an appetizer or spoon over Bibb lettuce leaves for a first-course salad.

Soups & Salads

Bouillabaisse
Makes 6 servings

2 cups water
1 package KNORR® Vegetable or Spring Vegetable recipe mix
1 bottle or can (8 to 10 ounces) clam juice
2 teaspoons tomato paste
½ teaspoon paprika
¼ teaspoon saffron threads (optional)
12 mussels or clams, well scrubbed
1½ pounds mixed seafood (cubed cod, snapper, scallops or
   shrimp)

❋ In 3-quart saucepan, bring water, recipe mix, clam juice, tomato paste, paprika and saffron to a boil over medium-high heat, stirring occasionally.

❋ Add mussels and seafood. Bring to a boil over high heat.

❋ Reduce heat to low and simmer 5 minutes or until shells open and seafood is cooked through and flakes easily when tested with a fork. Discard any unopened shells.

Prep Time: 15 minutes • *Cook Time:* 10 minutes

Mediterranean Shrimp Soup

Makes 6 servings

2 cans (14½ ounces each) chicken broth
1 can (about 14 ounces) diced tomatoes
1 can (8 ounces) tomato sauce
1 medium onion, chopped
½ medium green bell pepper, chopped
½ cup orange juice
½ cup dry white wine (optional)
1 jar (2½ ounces) sliced mushrooms
¼ cup sliced pitted black olives
2 cloves garlic, minced
1 teaspoon dried basil
2 bay leaves
¼ teaspoon fennel seeds, crushed
⅛ teaspoon black pepper
1 pound medium raw shrimp, peeled and deveined

Slow Cooker Directions

1. Place all ingredients except shrimp in slow cooker. Cover; cook on LOW 4 to 4½ hours or until vegetables are crisp-tender.

2. Stir in shrimp. Cover; cook 15 to 30 minutes or until shrimp are pink and opaque. Remove and discard bay leaves.

Note: For a heartier soup, add 1 pound of firm white fish, such as cod or haddock, cut into 1-inch pieces. Add the fish to the slow cooker 45 minutes before serving. Continue to cook, covered, on LOW.

Mediterranean Shrimp Soup

Gazpacho
Makes 10 to 12 servings

3 cups tomato juice
4 tomatoes, chopped
1 green bell pepper, chopped
1 cucumber, chopped
1 cup chopped celery
1 cup chopped green onions
3 tablespoons red wine vinegar
2 tablespoons **FILIPPO BERIO®** Olive Oil
1 tablespoon chopped fresh parsley
1 to 2 teaspoons salt
1 clove garlic, finely minced
    Freshly ground black pepper or hot pepper sauce

In large bowl, combine tomato juice, tomatoes, bell pepper, cucumber, celery, green onions, vinegar, olive oil, parsley, salt and garlic. Cover; refrigerate several hours or overnight before serving. Season to taste with black pepper or hot pepper sauce. Serve cold.

Gazpacho

Portuguese Potato & Greens Soup

Makes 4 (1½ cup) servings

2 tablespoons olive oil
1 cup chopped onion
1 cup chopped carrots
2 cloves garlic, minced
1 pound new red potatoes, unpeeled, cut into 1-inch pieces
2 cups water
1 can (about 14 ounces) chicken broth
½ teaspoon salt
½ pound chorizo sausage, casings removed
½ pound kale
   Salt and black pepper

1. Heat oil in large saucepan over medium heat. Add onion, carrots and garlic; cook and stir 5 to 6 minutes or until lightly browned. Add potatoes, water, chicken broth and salt. Bring to a boil. Reduce heat to low. Cover; simmer 10 to 15 minutes or until potatoes are tender. Cool slightly.

2. Meanwhile, heat large nonstick skillet over medium heat. Crumble chorizo into skillet. Cook and stir 5 to 6 minutes or until sausage is cooked through. Drain sausage on paper towels.

3. Wash kale; remove tough stems. Slice into thin shreds.

4. Lightly mash potato mixture in saucepan. Add sausage and kale; cook, uncovered, 4 to 5 minutes over medium heat until hot. Kale should be bright green and slightly crunchy. Season with salt and pepper.

Pappa al Pomodoro alla Papa Newman (Bread and Tomato Soup)

Makes 6 to 8 servings

¾ cup olive oil plus extra for drizzling on soup, divided
3 large cloves garlic, smashed
1 teaspoon dried sage
12 ounces stale Italian or French bread, thinly sliced, crusts removed (about 30 slices), divided
1 jar NEWMAN'S OWN® Bombolina Sauce (about 3 cups)
4 cups chicken broth
½ teaspoon hot red pepper flakes
½ teaspoon freshly ground black pepper
Freshly grated Parmesan cheese

1. In large skillet, heat ¼ cup oil over medium heat. Add garlic and sage and cook, stirring frequently, 1 to 2 minutes. Remove garlic from oil. Add ⅓ of bread slices and cook, turning once, until golden brown on both sides, 2 to 3 minutes per side. Remove from heat; repeat with remaining oil and bread.

2. In large heavy saucepan, heat Newman's Own® Bombolina Sauce and chicken broth over medium-high heat to boiling. Reduce heat to low. Add red pepper flakes, black pepper and bread; simmer, covered, 30 minutes. Remove from heat and let stand 30 minutes to 1 hour. Ladle into soup bowls. Drizzle lightly with olive oil and sprinkle with Parmesan cheese.

Winter Squash Soup
Makes 4 servings

1 tablespoon vegetable oil
1 tablespoon minced shallot or onion
2 cloves garlic, minced
3 fresh thyme sprigs
1 pinch dried rosemary
2 packages (10 ounces each) frozen winter (butternut) squash, thawed
1 cup chicken broth
3 tablespoons milk
  Sour cream (optional)

1. Heat vegetable oil in medium saucepan over medium heat. Add shallot, garlic, thyme and rosemary. Cook and stir 2 to 3 minutes or until shallot is tender. Add squash and chicken broth; bring to a boil. Add milk; stir until blended.

2. Remove thyme sprigs from soup. Transfer soup to blender or food processor; blend until smooth. (Add additional liquid to make soup thinner, if desired.) Top with dollop of sour cream.

Note: Add 2 tablespoons of fresh lemon juice to brighten the flavor of this hearty squash soup. Or, replace the sour cream with a toasted crouton. Garnish with chopped fresh cilantro or parsley.

Winter Squash Soup

Albóndigas

Makes 6 servings

1 pound ground beef
½ small onion, finely chopped
1 egg
¼ cup dry bread crumbs
1 tablespoon chili powder
1 teaspoon ground cumin
½ teaspoon salt
3 cans (about 14 ounces each) chicken broth
1 medium carrot, thinly sliced
1 package (10 ounces) frozen corn or thawed frozen leaf spinach
¼ cup dry sherry

1. Mix ground beef, onion, egg, bread crumbs, chili powder, cumin and salt in medium bowl until well blended. Place mixture on lightly oiled cutting board; pat evenly into 1-inch-thick square. Cut into 36 squares with sharp knife; shape each square into a ball.

2. Place meatballs slightly apart in single layer in microwavable container. Cover loosely with waxed paper. Cook on HIGH 3 minutes or until meatballs are just barely pink in center.

3. Meanwhile, combine broth and carrot in large saucepan. Cover; bring to a boil over high heat. Stir in corn and sherry. Transfer meatballs to broth with slotted spoon. Reduce heat to medium; simmer 3 to 4 minutes or until meatballs are cooked through.

Prep and Cook Time: 30 minutes

Note: For extra flavor, sprinkle chopped fresh cilantro over hot soup.

Albóndigas

Mediterranean Fish Soup
Makes 4 servings

4 ounces uncooked pastina or other small pasta
1 tablespoon olive oil
¾ cup chopped onion
2 cloves garlic, minced
1 teaspoon fennel seeds
1 can (about 14 ounces) stewed tomatoes
1 can (about 14 ounces) chicken broth
1 tablespoon minced fresh parsley
½ teaspoon black pepper
¼ teaspoon ground turmeric
8 ounces firm, white-fleshed fish, cut into 1-inch pieces
3 ounces small raw shrimp, peeled and deveined

1. Cook pasta according to package directions. Drain; set aside.

2. Heat oil in large nonstick saucepan over medium heat. Add onion, garlic and fennel seeds; cook 3 minutes or until onion is tender.

3. Stir in tomatoes, chicken broth, parsley, pepper and turmeric. Bring to a boil; reduce heat and simmer 10 minutes. Add fish and cook 1 minute. Add shrimp and cook until shrimp just begin to turn pink and opaque.

4. Divide pasta among 4 bowls; ladle soup over pasta.

Mediterranean Fish Soup

Marinated Tomato Salad

Makes 8 servings

1½ cups tarragon vinegar or white wine vinegar
½ teaspoon salt
¼ cup finely chopped shallots
2 tablespoons finely chopped chives
2 tablespoons fresh lemon juice
¼ teaspoon white pepper
2 tablespoons extra-virgin olive oil
6 plum tomatoes, quartered vertically
2 large yellow tomatoes,* sliced horizontally into ½-inch thick slices
16 red cherry tomatoes, halved vertically
16 small yellow pear tomatoes,* halved vertically
    Sunflower sprouts (optional)

Substitute 10 plum tomatoes, quartered vertically, for yellow tomatoes and yellow pear tomatoes, if desired.

1. Combine vinegar and salt in large bowl; stir until salt is completely dissolved. Add shallots, chives, lemon juice and pepper; mix well. Slowly whisk in oil until well blended.

2. Add tomatoes to marinade; toss well. Cover; let stand at room temperature 2 to 3 hours.

3. To serve, divide tomatoes evenly among 8 salad plates. Garnish each plate with sunflower sprouts.

Marinated Tomato Salad

Hearty Antipasto Salad

Makes 12 servings (10 cups)

2 jars (6 ounces each) artichoke hearts
1 pound fresh mozzarella cheese, cut into ½-inch cubes (3 cups)
1 can (14 ounces) baby corn spears, drained
2 jars (4½ ounces each) button mushrooms, drained
1 jar (7 ounces) roasted red peppers, drained and diced
1 cup medium pitted black olives
½ cup chopped fresh parsley
3 tablespoons *Frank's® RedHot®* Original Cayenne Pepper Sauce
2 tablespoons olive oil
2 tablespoons balsamic vinegar
2 cloves garlic, pressed
  Lettuce leaves (optional)

1. Drain artichoke hearts, reserve liquid. Combine cheese, corn, artichoke hearts, mushrooms, roasted peppers, olives and parsley in large bowl; set aside.

2. Whisk liquid from artichokes, *Frank's RedHot* Sauce, oil, vinegar and garlic in small bowl. Pour over cheese mixture; toss to coat evenly.

3. Cover; refrigerate 30 minutes. Toss just before serving. Serve on lettuce-lined plates, if desired.

Prep Time: 20 minutes • *Chill Time:* 30 minutes

Orange-Shrimp Salad
with Ripe Olives in Sherry Vinaigrette

Makes 8 servings

1 (6-ounce) can whole, pitted California Ripe Olives
2 pounds large shrimp, peeled, deveined, boiled, chilled
4 cups peeled navel orange slices
2 teaspoons orange zest
½ cup red wine vinaigrette dressing
2 tablespoons dry sherry
2 teaspoons minced garlic
2 teaspoons sugar
12 cups mixed field greens
½ cup minced scallion greens

Combine first four ingredients in large bowl. Mix well. Combine vinaigrette dressing and sherry with garlic and sugar. Pour over shrimp mixture. Toss well. Adjust seasoning with salt and pepper. Arrange 1½ cups field greens on each plate. Top with 1 cup of salad mixture and sprinkle with scallion greens.

Favorite recipe from **California Olive Industry**

Spinach & Prosciutto Salad
Makes 4 servings

Salad
- 12 slices of prosciutto
- 6 small plum tomatoes, halved
- 4 tablespoons FILIPPO BERIO® Extra-Virgin Olive Oil
- Freshly ground black pepper
- 7 ounces of baby spinach leaves, washed and dried well
- 7 ounces of baby fresh asparagus, blanched for two minutes and chilled

Dressing
- 2 tablespoons FILIPPO BERIO® Extra-Virgin Olive Oil
- 2 tablespoons fresh lemon juice
- 2 tablespoons fresh basil, finely shredded
- A little sugar to taste
- Parmesan shavings, for garnish

Preheat the oven to 350°F. Put the prosciutto and tomatoes cut side up onto a baking tray. Drizzle with the olive oil and season well. Cook for 25 minutes or until just soft. Arrange the spinach and asparagus onto the serving plates and top with the tomatoes and prosciutto. Mix all salad dressing ingredients together except Parmesan; season to taste. Pour over the salad just before serving. Garnish with Parmesan.

Prep Time: 12 to 15 minutes • *Cook Time:* 25 minutes

Spinach & Prosciutto Salad

Hearty Italian Minestrone
Makes 10 servings

    7 cups water
2½ tablespoons HERB-OX® sodium free beef flavored bouillon
    2 cups coarsely chopped cabbage
    1 (14½-ounce) can diced tomatoes with basil, garlic and oregano
    1 medium onion, chopped
    1 medium carrot, halved lengthwise and diagonally sliced
    1 tablespoon Italian seasoning
1½ cups frozen French cut green beans
    1 zucchini, halved lengthwise and quartered
    ½ cup ditalini or small shell pasta
    1 (15-ounce) can red kidney beans, drained
    1 cup HORMEL® Sliced Pepperoni, quartered
      Garlic salt and pepper, to taste
      Refrigerated prepared pesto (optional)
      Shredded Parmesan cheese (optional)

In large stockpot, combine first seven ingredients. Bring to a boil. Reduce heat to low and simmer, partially covered, for 20 minutes. Add green beans, zucchini and pasta. Simmer, uncovered for an additional 15 minutes or until vegetables and pasta are tender. Stir in beans and pepperoni. Heat until warmed through, about 2 minutes. Season to taste with garlic salt and pepper. If desired, serve with pesto and Parmesan cheese.

Prep Time: 20 minutes • *Total Time:* 1¼ hours

Tuscan White Bean Soup

Makes 8 to 10 servings

  6 ounces bacon, diced
 10 cups chicken broth
  1 bag (16 ounces) dried Great Northern beans, rinsed
  1 can (about 14 ounces) diced tomatoes
  1 large onion, chopped
  3 carrots, chopped
  4 cloves garlic, minced
  1 fresh rosemary sprig *or* 1 teaspoon dried rosemary
  1 teaspoon black pepper

Slow Cooker Directions

1. Cook bacon in medium skillet over medium-high heat until crisp; drain on paper towels. Transfer to 5-quart slow cooker. Add broth, beans, tomatoes, onion, carrots, garlic, rosemary sprig and pepper.

2. Cover; cook on LOW 8 hours or until beans are tender. Remove and discard rosemary sprig before serving.

Serving Suggestion: Place slices of toasted Italian bread in bottom of individual soup bowls. Drizzle with olive oil. Ladle soup over bread and serve.

Grilled Tri-Colored Pepper Salad

Makes 4 to 6 servings

1 each large red, yellow and green bell pepper, cut into halves or quarters
⅓ cup extra-virgin olive oil
3 tablespoons balsamic vinegar
2 cloves garlic, minced
¼ teaspoon salt
¼ teaspoon black pepper
⅓ cup crumbled goat cheese (about 1½ ounces)
¼ cup thinly sliced fresh basil leaves

1. Prepare grill for direct cooking.

2. Place bell peppers, skin-side down, on grid. Grill bell peppers, on covered grill, over hot coals 10 to 12 minutes or until skin is charred. Place charred bell peppers in paper bag. Close bag; set aside to cool 10 to 15 minutes. Remove skin with paring knife; discard skin.

3. Place bell peppers in shallow glass serving dish. Combine oil, vinegar, garlic, salt and black pepper in small bowl; whisk until well combined. Pour over bell peppers. Let stand 30 minutes at room temperature. (Or, cover and refrigerate up to 24 hours. Bring bell peppers to room temperature before serving.)

4. Sprinkle bell peppers with cheese and basil just before serving.

Grilled Tri-Colored Pepper Salad

Easy Niçoise Salad

Makes 4 servings

Lettuce leaves
2 medium tomatoes, thinly sliced
1½ cups sliced cooked potatoes
1¼ cups cooked green beans
1 (7-ounce) STARKIST Flavor Fresh Pouch® Tuna
(Albacore or Chunk Light)
4 slices red or white onion, separated into rings
½ cup sliced pitted ripe olives
1 hard-cooked egg, sliced
4 whole anchovies (optional)

Vinegar 'n' Oil Dressing
½ cup white vinegar
⅓ cup vegetable oil
1 tablespoon chopped parsley
½ teaspoon salt
¼ teaspoon pepper

On a large platter or 4 individual salad plates, arrange lettuce leaves. Arrange tomatoes, potatoes, beans, tuna, onion rings, olives and egg in a decorative design. Garnish with anchovies, if desired.

For dressing, in a shaker jar combine remaining ingredients. Cover and shake until well blended. Drizzle some of the dressing over salad; serve remaining dressing.

Prep Time: 20 minutes

Easy Niçoise Salad

Orzo Salad
with Ripe Olives and Pine Nuts
Makes 8 servings

2 cups sliced California Ripe Olives
1 cup diced red bell pepper (¼ inch)
1 cup diced yellow bell pepper (¼ inch)
1 cup diced green bell pepper (¼ inch)
½ cup minced scallions
¼ cup capers
2 (1-pound) packages orzo pasta, cooked, chilled
1 cup herbed white wine vinaigrette dressing
½ cup pine nuts, toasted

Combine first six ingredients in large bowl. Mix well. Add orzo pasta and vinaigrette dressing. Toss well. Sprinkle with toasted pine nuts.

Favorite recipe from **California Olive Industry**

Tuscan Bread Salad (Panzanella Salad)
Makes 9 (1-cup) servings

1½ pounds tomatoes, chopped (about 4 large)
1 cucumber, peeled and chopped
1 small red onion, thinly sliced
1 cup WISH-BONE® Italian Dressing
3 tablespoons drained capers
4 cups day-old, cubed Italian bread (about 6 ounces)

In large bowl, combine all ingredients except bread. Add bread and toss until evenly coated. Chill at least 1 hour before serving.

Prep Time: 10 minutes • *Chill Time:* 1 hour

Warm Mushroom and Goat Cheese Salad

Makes 6 servings

  6 cups mixed salad greens
¼ cup extra-virgin olive oil
12 ounces white mushrooms, trimmed and sliced (about 4½ cups)
½ pound oyster mushrooms, trimmed and sliced (about 4½ cups)
¼ cup pine nuts
  2 large shallots, chopped
  3 tablespoons sherry vinegar
  1 teaspoon sugar
  1 teaspoon salt
¼ ground black pepper
  3 ounces crumbled goat cheese or blue cheese (about ¾ cup)

Arrange 1 cup greens on each of 6 plates. In a large skillet, heat oil over
high heat. Add white mushrooms; cook and stir until mushrooms are
browned and liquid has evaporated, about 10 minutes. Add oyster
mushrooms, pine nuts and shallots; cook until mushrooms soften, about
1 minute. Stir in sherry vinegar, sugar, salt and black pepper. Divide
mixture over greens. Sprinkle goat cheese over mushrooms; serve
immediately. Garnish with finely shredded basil leaves, if desired.

Favorite recipe from **Mushroom Council**

Magnificent Seafood

Grilled Sea Bass
with Ripe Olive 'n Caper Salsa

Makes 8 servings

1 cup sliced **California Ripe Olives**
½ cup seeded, diced **Roma tomatoes**
½ cup chopped **oil-packed sun-dried tomatoes**
¼ cup minced **red onion**
¼ cup chopped **fresh basil**
3 tablespoons **capers**
2 tablespoons chopped **fresh parsley**
2 tablespoons **Balsamic-style vinaigrette dressing**
1 teaspoon minced **garlic**
8 (6-ounce) **sea bass or other white fish fillets**
 Olive oil

Preheat grill or broiler. Combine all ingredients except sea
bass and olive oil in large bowl. Mix well. Adjust seasoning
with salt and pepper. Cover and chill. Brush both sides of
fillets with olive oil and season with salt and pepper. Broil or
grill until fish is firm to the touch, about 5 minutes on each
side. Serve each fillet with about ¼ cup of Ripe Olive 'n
Caper Salsa.

Favorite recipe from **California Olive Industry**

Halibut with Roasted Pepper Sauce

Makes 4 servings

Roasted Pepper Sauce (recipe follows)
1 medium onion, thinly sliced
1 clove garlic, minced
1 halibut fillet, skinned (about 1½ pounds)

1. Prepare Roasted Pepper Sauce; set aside.

2. Preheat oven to 425°F. Spray shallow baking dish with nonstick cooking spray. Cover bottom of baking dish with onion and garlic. Top with fish and sauce.

3. Bake 20 minutes or until fish flakes easily when tested with fork.

Roasted Pepper Sauce

Makes about ¾ cup

1 can (7 ounces) chopped green chiles, drained
1 jar (7 ounces) roasted red peppers, drained
⅔ cup chicken broth

Combine ingredients in food processor or blender; process until smooth.

Halibut with Roasted Pepper Sauce

Moroccan Swordfish

Makes 4 servings

  4 swordfish steaks, about 1 inch thick
  1 tablespoon fresh lemon juice
  1 tablespoon apple cider vinegar
2½ teaspoons garlic-flavored vegetable oil
  1 teaspoon ground ginger
  1 teaspoon paprika
  ½ teaspoon ground cumin
  ½ teaspoon hot chili oil
  ¼ teaspoon salt
  ¼ teaspoon ground coriander
  ⅛ teaspoon black pepper
    Hot cooked couscous

1. Place swordfish in single layer in medium shallow dish. Combine lemon juice, vinegar, garlic-flavored oil, ginger, paprika, cumin, chili oil, salt, coriander and pepper in small bowl. Pour over swordfish; turn to coat both sides. Cover; refrigerate 40 minutes, turning once.

2. Prepare grill for direct cooking. Discard marinade; grill swordfish, uncovered, over medium-hot coals 8 to 10 minutes or until swordfish is opaque and flakes easily when tested with fork, turning once. Serve with couscous.

Moroccan Swordfish

Paella

Makes 6 servings

       1 pound raw littleneck clams
       8 to 10 ounces raw sea scallops
       6 ounces medium raw shrimp
       2 tablespoons olive oil, divided
    3¼ cups chicken broth, divided
       1 medium onion, finely chopped
       3 cloves garlic, chopped
       2 cups uncooked long-grain white rice
       1 teaspoon dried thyme
     ½ teaspoon crushed saffron threads
       1 pint (about 12 ounces) cherry tomatoes, halved
       1 cup frozen petite peas, thawed
       1 tablespoon chopped fresh parsley

1. Discard any clams that remain open when tapped with fingers. To clean clams, scrub with stiff brush under cold running water. Soak clams in mixture of ⅓ cup salt to 1 gallon of water 20 minutes. Drain water; repeat 2 more times. Slice scallops in half crosswise into rounds. Peel shrimp, leaving tails on; devein.

2. Heat 1 tablespoon oil over medium-high heat in large saucepan. Add shrimp; cook 3 minutes or until shrimp turn pink and opaque, stirring occasionally. Transfer to bowl; keep warm. Add scallops to saucepan; cook 2 minutes or until scallops are opaque. Transfer to bowl with shrimp. Add clams and ¼ cup broth to pan. Cover; boil 2 to 8 minutes or until clams open. Transfer clams and broth to bowl with shrimp and scallops; discard any unopened clams.

continued on page 78

Paella

Paella, continued

3. Heat remaining 1 tablespoon oil in same saucepan. Add onion and garlic; cook and stir 4 minutes or until tender. Add rice; cook and stir 2 minutes. Add remaining 3 cups broth, thyme and saffron; reduce heat to medium-low. Cover; simmer 15 minutes or until rice is tender. Stir in tomatoes, peas and parsley. Stir in seafood and accumulated juices. Cover; remove from heat. Let stand 3 to 5 minutes or until seafood is hot.

Orzo Pasta with Shrimp
Makes 4 servings

         8 ounces uncooked orzo pasta
         3 tablespoons plus ½ teaspoon **FILIPPO BERIO®** Olive Oil, divided
         3 cloves garlic, minced
    1¼ pounds raw small shrimp, shelled and deveined
    1½ medium tomatoes, chopped
         2 tablespoons chopped fresh cilantro
         2 tablespoons chopped fresh Italian parsley
            Juice of 1 lemon
         2 ounces feta cheese, crumbled
            Salt and freshly ground black pepper

Cook pasta according to package directions until al dente (tender but still firm). Drain. Toss with ½ teaspoon olive oil; set aside. Heat remaining 3 tablespoons olive oil in large skillet over medium heat until hot. Add garlic; cook and stir 2 to 3 minutes or until golden. Add shrimp; cook and stir 3 to 5 minutes or until shrimp are opaque. *(Do not overcook.)* Stir in pasta. Add tomatoes, cilantro, parsley and lemon juice. Sprinkle with feta cheese. Season to taste with salt and pepper.

Tuna Steaks with Tomatoes & Olives

2 tablespoons olive oil, divided
1 small onion, quartered and sliced
1 clove garlic, minced
1⅓ cups chopped tomatoes
¼ cup sliced drained black olives
2 anchovy fillets, finely chopped (optional)
2 tablespoons chopped fresh basil
¼ teaspoon salt, divided
⅛ teaspoon red pepper flakes
4 tuna steaks (¾ inch thick)
   Black pepper
¼ cup toasted pine nuts (optional)

1. Heat 1 tablespoon oil in large skillet over medium heat. Add onion;
cook and stir 4 minutes. Add garlic; cook and stir about 30 seconds.
Add tomatoes; cook 3 minutes, stirring occasionally. Stir in olives,
anchovies, if desired, basil, ⅛ teaspoon salt and pepper flakes. Cook
until hot and most of liquid had evaporated.

2. Meanwhile, sprinkle tuna with remaining ⅛ teaspoon salt and black
pepper. Heat remaining 1 tablespoon oil in another large skillet over
medium high heat. Cook tuna 2 minutes per side or until tuna is
medium-rare. Serve with tomato mixture. Garnish with pine nuts.

Shrimp Scampi

Makes 4 servings

⅓ cup clarified butter*
4 tablespoons minced garlic
1½ pounds large raw shrimp, peeled and deveined
6 green onions, thinly sliced
¼ cup dry white wine
2 tablespoons lemon juice
8 large sprigs fresh parsley, finely chopped
Salt and black pepper
Lemon wedges (optional)

To clarify butter, melt butter over low heat. Skim off the white foam that forms on top, then strain clear golden butter through cheesecloth into container. Discard milky residue at the bottom of pan. Clarified butter will keep, covered, in refrigerator for up to 2 months.

1. Heat clarified butter in large skillet over medium heat. Add garlic; cook and stir 1 to 2 minutes or until soft but not brown. Add shrimp, onions, wine and lemon juice; cook 2 to 4 minutes or until shrimp turn pink and opaque, stirring occasionally. Do not overcook.

2. Add chopped parsley; season with salt and pepper. Garnish with lemon.

Note: Scampi is the Italian name for the tail portion of certain types of shrimp, such as large prawns. In the United States, the term "scampi" often refers to shrimp served in a sauce of garlic and butter.

Shrimp Scampi

Mediterranean Cod

Makes about 4 servings

1 bag (16 ounces) **BIRDS EYE®** frozen Broccoli, Green Beans,
    Pearl Onions and Red Peppers
1 can (14½ ounces) stewed tomatoes
½ teaspoon dried basil leaves
1 pound cod fillets, cut into serving pieces
½ cup orange juice, divided
2 tablespoons all-purpose flour
¼ cup sliced black olives (optional)

❋ Combine vegetables, tomatoes and basil in large skillet. Bring to boil over medium-high heat.

❋ Place cod on vegetables. Pour ¼ cup orange juice over fish. Cover and cook 5 to 7 minutes or until fish is tender and flakes with fork.

❋ Remove cod and keep warm. Blend flour with remaining ¼ cup orange juice; stir into skillet. Cook until liquid is thickened and vegetables are coated.

❋ Serve fish with vegetables; sprinkle with olives.

Prep Time: 5 minutes • ***Cook Time:*** 15 minutes

Serving Suggestion: **Serve with rice or couscous.**

Mediterranean Cod

Spicy Shrimp Puttanesca

Makes 4 servings

   8 ounces uncooked linguine, capellini or spaghetti
   1 tablespoon olive oil
12 ounces medium raw shrimp, peeled and deveined
   4 cloves garlic, minced
¾ teaspoon red pepper flakes
   1 cup finely chopped onion
   1 can (about 14 ounces) stewed tomatoes
   2 tablespoons tomato paste
   2 tablespoons chopped pitted kalamata or black olives
   1 tablespoon drained capers
¼ cup chopped fresh basil or parsley

1. Cook linguine according to package directions. Drain; set aside.

2. Meanwhile, heat oil in large nonstick skillet over medium high heat. Add shrimp, garlic and pepper flakes; cook and stir 3 to 4 minutes or until shrimp are pink and opaque. Transfer shrimp mixture to bowl with slotted spoon; set aside.

3. Add onion to same skillet; cook over medium heat 5 minutes, stirring occasionally. Add tomatoes, tomato paste, olives and capers; simmer, uncovered, 5 minutes.

4. Return shrimp mixture to skillet; simmer 1 minute. Stir in basil; simmer 1 minute. Place linguine in large serving bowl; top with shrimp mixture.

Spicy Shrimp Puttanesca

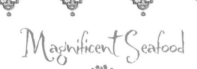
Steamed Clams in Wine Broth

Makes 3 to 4 servings

    6 tablespoons margarine, melted
    ¾ cup dry white wine
    ¾ cup water
1½ tablespoons chopped fresh parsley
    ¼ teaspoon hot pepper sauce
    4 pounds cherrystone or little neck clams, scrubbed

Bring margarine, wine, water, parsley and hot pepper sauce to a boil in bottom of steamer. Arrange clams on steamer rack and place in steamer. Cover. Steam about 8 minutes or until clams open. Discard any clams that do not open. Divide clams into 3 or 4 serving bowls. Ladle broth over them.

Favorite recipe from **National Fisheries Institute**

Mussels Steamed in White Wine

Makes 2 servings

¼ cup olive oil
1 onion, chopped
¼ cup chopped celery
2 cloves garlic, minced
1 bay leaf
½ teaspoon dried basil leaves, crushed
1 pound raw mussels, scrubbed
1 cup dry white wine

Heat oil in large saucepan. Add onion, celery, garlic, bay leaf and basil. Add mussels and wine; stir well. Cover and steam 4 to 6 minutes or until mussels open. Discard any mussels that do not open. Garnish with chopped parsley; serve.

Favorite recipe from **National Fisheries Institute**

Steamed Clams in Wine Broth

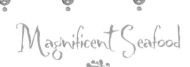

Magnificent Seafood

Garlic Shrimp with Wilted Spinach

Makes about 4 servings

  2 teaspoons BERTOLLI® Olive Oil
  1 pound uncooked medium shrimp, peeled and deveined
  ¼ cup diagonally sliced green onions
  2 tablespoons sherry or dry white wine (optional)
  1 envelope LIPTON® RECIPE SECRETS® Savory Herb
      with Garlic Soup Mix*
1½ cups water
  1 large tomato, diced
  2 cups fresh trimmed spinach leaves (about 4 ounces)
  ¼ cup chopped unsalted cashews (optional)

Also terrific with LIPTON® RECIPE SECRETS® Golden Onion Soup Mix.

In 12-inch skillet, heat oil over medium heat and cook shrimp 2 minutes
or until pink. Remove and set aside.

In same skillet, cook green onions, stirring occasionally, 2 minutes
or until slightly soft. Add sherry and bring to a boil over high heat,
stirring frequently. Stir in soup mix blended with water. Bring to a boil
over high heat. Reduce heat to low and simmer 5 minutes or until sauce
is thickened. Stir in tomato and spinach. Simmer, covered, stirring once,
3 minutes or until spinach is cooked. Return shrimp to skillet and cook
1 minute or until heated through. Sprinkle with cashews.

Menu Suggestion: Serve with hot cooked rice and fresh fruit for dessert.

Garlic Shrimp with Wilted Spinach

Frutti di Mare

Makes 8 servings

¼ cup olive oil
1 large onion, chopped
6 large mushrooms, chopped (about 4 ounces)
2 cloves garlic, finely chopped
1 jar (1 pound 10 ounces) RAGÚ® ROBUSTO!® Pasta Sauce
½ cup chicken broth
⅓ cup lemon juice
1 dozen littleneck clams, well scrubbed
1 dozen mussels, beards removed and well scrubbed
1 lobster (about 1¼ pounds), cut into 2-inch pieces
1 pound bay scallops
1 box (16 ounces) spaghetti, cooked and drained

In large saucepan, heat olive oil over medium-high heat and cook onion, mushrooms and garlic, stirring occasionally, 5 minutes or until tender. Stir in Pasta Sauce, chicken broth and lemon juice. Bring to a boil over high heat.

Reduce heat and simmer covered, stirring occasionally, 20 minutes. Add clams and mussels and simmer covered 5 minutes or until shells open. Remove shellfish as they open. (Discard any unopened clams or mussels.) Add lobster and scallops and simmer 3 minutes or until done. To serve, arrange shellfish over hot spaghetti and top with Sauce. Sprinkle, if desired, with chopped parsley.

Prep Time: 20 minutes • ***Cook Time:*** 35 minutes

Frutti di Mare

Tunisian Fish with Couscous

Makes 6 servings

¼ cup olive oil
2 cups chopped onions
8 cloves garlic, minced
2 tablespoons tomato paste
1 tablespoon ground cumin
1 tablespoon paprika
½ teaspoon ground cinnamon
8 cups chicken broth, divided
1½ pounds small potatoes, quartered
5 medium carrots, peeled and cut into 2×¼-inch strips
1 large red bell pepper, seeded and cut into ½-inch strips
1 can (about 15 ounces) chickpeas, rinsed and drained
½ teaspoon salt
6 grouper fillets (about 5 ounces each)
2 cups uncooked couscous

1. Heat oil in large saucepan over medium heat; add onions and garlic. Cook and stir 3 minutes or until onions are tender. Stir in tomato paste, cumin, paprika and cinnamon. Cook 1 minute, stirring constantly.

2. Add 5 cups chicken broth to onion mixture. Increase heat to high. Bring mixture to a boil. Reduce heat to low; simmer, covered, 10 minutes. Add potatoes to broth; simmer, covered, 10 minutes. Add carrots, bell pepper, chickpeas and salt to broth; simmer, covered, 5 minutes.

3. Rinse fish fillets; pat dry with paper towels. Cut into 2×1-inch strips. Add fish to broth; simmer, covered, 5 to 7 minutes until fish flakes easily when tested with fork.

4. Bring remaining 3 cups broth to a boil in medium saucepan over medium-high heat. Stir in couscous. Remove from heat. Cover; let stand 5 minutes or until liquid is absorbed. Fluff with fork.

5. Spoon couscous into shallow soup plates. Top with fish and vegetables.

Tunisian Fish with Couscous

Squid Mediterranean

Makes 4 servings

2 pounds cleaned whole squid (body and tentacles)
1 tablespoon olive oil
¾ cup finely chopped onion
1 clove garlic, minced
2 (16-ounce) cans Italian-style tomatoes, drained and chopped
3 tablespoons sliced black olives
1 tablespoon capers
½ teaspoon dried oregano
¼ teaspoon dried marjoram
⅛ teaspoon crushed red pepper

Cut body of squid into ½-inch slices; set aside. Heat olive oil in a large skillet; add onion and garlic. Cook until onion is tender. Add squid and remaining ingredients. Bring to a boil. Cover, reduce heat and simmer 30 minutes or until squid is tender.

Prep and Cook Time: about 45 minutes

Favorite recipe from **National Fisheries Institute**

Squid Mediterranean

Orange-Glazed Roasted Salmon and Fennel

Makes 4 to 6 servings

1 tablespoon FILIPPO BERIO® Extra-Virgin or Pure Olive Oil,
    plus additional for the baking pan
2 to 3 navel oranges
1½ teaspoons salt
2 large bulbs fennel
1 large salmon fillet (2 to 2½ pounds)

Preheat the oven to 400°F. Coat a 16×10-inch baking pan with oil.

Grate 1 tablespoon orange zest. Squeeze oranges to get ½ cup juice. In a small bowl whisk the zest, juice, oil, and salt. Trim the fennel. Mince about 2 tablespoons of the feathery leaves; set aside. (The remaining leaves may be reserved for salads or other recipes.) Cut bulbs lengthwise into quarters. Cut out and discard the cores. Cut the fennel into thick slices. Place the fennel in the baking pan. Drizzle with half of the juice mixture. Toss to coat. Place in the oven for about 20 minutes, stirring occasionally, or until lightly browned. Remove the pan from the oven. Clear a space in the center and lay the salmon diagonally in the pan, skin side down. Drizzle with the remaining juice mixture. Spread to coat the fish. Place in the oven and roast for about 15 minutes, or until the salmon is opaque in the center.

Orange-Glazed Roasted Salmon and Fennel

Easy Paella

Makes 4 servings

1 medium onion, cut into halves and chopped
1 large red or green bell pepper, sliced
1 clove garlic, minced
2 tablespoons vegetable oil
1 can (16 ounces) tomatoes with juice, cut up
1 package (9 ounces) frozen artichoke hearts, cut into quarters
½ cup dry white wine
½ teaspoon dried thyme, crushed
¼ teaspoon salt
⅛ teaspoon saffron or turmeric
2 cups cooked rice
1 cup frozen peas
½ pound large shrimp, peeled and deveined
1 (3-ounce)STARKIST Flavor Fresh Pouch® Tuna
    (Albacore or Chunk Light)

In a large skillet sauté onion, bell pepper and garlic in oil for 3 minutes.
Stir in tomatoes with juice, artichoke hearts, wine and seasonings. Bring
to a boil; reduce heat. Simmer for 10 minutes. Stir in rice, peas, shrimp
and tuna. Cook for 3 to 5 minutes more or until shrimp turn pink and
mixture is heated.

Prep Time: 30 minutes

Easy Paella

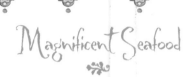

Eggplant & Shrimp over Fusilli

Makes 6 servings

2 tablespoons olive oil, divided
1 large eggplant (about 1½ pounds), peeled and cut into 1-inch cubes
    (about 6 cups)
⅔ cup water, divided
1 medium onion, chopped
2 cloves garlic, finely chopped
¾ teaspoon salt
¼ teaspoon ground black pepper
1 jar (1 pound 10 ounces) RAGÚ® Light Pasta Sauce
8 ounces uncooked shrimp, peeled and deveined
1 box (16 ounces) fusilli pasta or spaghetti, cooked and drained
1 cup crumbled feta cheese (optional)

In 12-inch nonstick skillet, heat 1 tablespoon olive oil over medium heat and cook eggplant with ⅓ cup water, covered, stirring occasionally, 15 minutes or until eggplant is tender. Remove eggplant and set aside.

In same skillet, heat remaining 1 tablespoon olive oil over medium heat and cook onion, garlic, salt and pepper 2 minutes or until onion is tender. Stir in Pasta Sauce, remaining ⅓ cup water and eggplant. Reduce heat to low and simmer covered, stirring occasionally, 6 minutes. Stir in shrimp and simmer, stirring occasionally, 4 minutes or until shrimp turn pink. Serve over hot pasta and garnish with crumbled feta cheese, if desired.

Eggplant & Shrimp over Fusilli

Spicy Tuna Empanadas

Makes 8 servings

1 (3-ounce) STARKIST Flavor Fresh Pouch® Tuna
   (Albacore or Chunk Light)
1 can (4 ounces) diced green chilies, drained
1 can (2¼ ounces) sliced ripe olives, drained
½ cup shredded sharp Cheddar cheese
1 chopped hard-cooked egg
   Salt and pepper to taste
¼ teaspoon hot pepper sauce
¼ cup medium thick and chunky salsa
2 packages (15 ounces each) refrigerated pie crusts
   Additional salsa

In medium bowl, place tuna, chilies, olives, cheese, egg, salt, pepper and
hot pepper sauce; toss lightly with fork. Add ¼ cup salsa and toss again;
set aside. Following directions on package, unfold pie crusts (roll out
slightly with rolling pin if you prefer thinner crust); cut 4 circles,
4 inches each, out of each crust. Place 8 circles on foil-covered baking
sheets; wet edge of each circle with water. Top each circle with ¼ cup
lightly packed tuna mixture. Top with remaining circles, stretching
pastry slightly to fit; press edges together and crimp with fork. Cut slits
in top crust to vent. Bake in 425°F oven 15 to 18 minutes or until golden
brown. Cool slightly. Serve with additional salsa.

Spicy Tuna Empanadas

Shellfish Fettuccine
with Ripe Olives and Garlic

Makes 8 servings

¼ cup olive oil
3 pounds diced Roma tomatoes
½ cup capers
¼ cup chopped anchovies
2 tablespoons chopped garlic
3 pounds peeled, deveined medium shrimp
1 (6-ounce) can pitted whole California Ripe Olives
2 (16-ounce) packages fettuccine pasta, cooked and kept warm
2 tablespoons olive oil
½ cup chopped flat-leaf parsley

Heat olive oil in shallow heavy pot. Add tomatoes, capers, anchovies and garlic. Cook over medium heat until tomatoes release juices and mixture thickens, about 5 to 10 minutes. Add shrimp and olives. Simmer until shrimp is firm, about 4 to 5 minutes. Toss hot pasta with olive oil. Add shrimp mixture to hot pasta and toss well. Portion onto plates or shallow bowls. Sprinkle with chopped parsley.

Favorite recipe from **California Olive Industry**

Broiled Trout with Piñon Butter

Makes 4 servings

 4 whole trout (each about 8 ounces), cleaned
 ¼ cup vegetable oil
 ¼ cup dry white wine
 2 tablespoons minced chives
 2 tablespoons chopped fresh parsley
 ½ teaspoon salt
 ⅛ teaspoon black pepper
 ¼ cup butter, softened
 ¼ cup pine nuts, finely chopped
 1 lemon, cut into wedges (optional)

1. Place trout in large heavy-duty resealable food storage bag. Whisk oil, wine, chives, parsley, salt and pepper in small bowl. Pour over fish; seal bag. Marinate 30 minutes or refrigerate up to 2 hours, turning bag occasionally to distribute marinade.

2. Combine butter and pine nuts; stir until well blended. Cover; let stand at room temperature until ready to use.

3. Preheat broiler; spray broiling pan with nonstick cooking spray. Remove fish from marinade; reserve marinade. Place fish on broiling pan. Broil 4 to 6 inches from heat 4 minutes; turn fish over. Brush with marinade; continue broiling 4 to 6 minutes or until fish turns opaque and just begins to flake. Transfer fish to serving platter. Place a dollop of reserved butter mixture on each fish. Garnish with lemon wedges.

Note: If you prefer to grill trout, place fish in a hinged wire basket and grill, uncovered, 4 to 6 inches above low-glowing coals.

Grilled Swordfish Sicilian Style

Makes 4 to 6 servings

 3 tablespoons extra-virgin olive oil
 1 clove garlic, minced
 2 tablespoons lemon juice
 ¾ teaspoon salt
 ⅛ teaspoon black pepper
 3 tablespoons capers, drained
 1 tablespoon chopped fresh oregano or basil
1½ pounds swordfish steaks (¾ inch thick)

1. Prepare grill for direct cooking.

2. Heat olive oil in small saucepan over low heat. Add garlic; cook 1 minute. Remove from heat; cool slightly. Whisk in lemon juice, salt and pepper until salt is dissolved. Stir in capers and oregano.

3. Place swordfish on oiled grid over medium heat. Grill 7 to 8 minutes, turning once, or until fish is opaque in center. Serve fish with lemon juice mixture.

Note: Capers are the small, pea-sized bud of a flower from the caper bush. These pickled green buds are used to add pungency and a hint of saltiness to Mediterranean sauces, dips and relishes. They can be found in the condiment section of the supermarket.

Grilled Swordfish Sicilian Style

Meaty Entrées

Lamb Kabobs Wrapped in Pita

Makes 4 to 6 servings

1½ pounds boneless leg of Australian Lamb, cut into 1-inch cubes
1 tablespoon and 1 teaspoon fresh thyme
2 cloves minced garlic, divided
1 teaspoon salt
½ teaspoon freshly ground pepper
1 cup plain whole-milk yogurt
1 tablespoon fresh lemon juice
4 to 6 large pitas
  Garnishes: chopped lettuce, tabbouleh or diced tomato

1. Place lamb in large bowl. Combine 1 tablespoon thyme, half the garlic, salt and pepper. Add to lamb and toss well. Cover and leave for 20 minutes to allow the flavors to infuse. Thread onto metal or pre-soaked wooden skewers.

2. Place yogurt in small bowl; add remaining thyme, garlic and lemon juice; mix well. Season with salt and pepper.

3. Broil or barbecue kabobs over medium-high heat until cooked as desired, about 4 to 5 minutes each side for medium rare.

4. Toast pitas lightly on grill until just warmed; top with lettuce, tabbouleh or tomato. Remove lamb from skewers; place on salad. Drizzle with yogurt; wrap firmly into a roll.

Favorite recipe from **Meat and Livestock Australia**

Moroccan Pork Tagine

Makes 4 servings

1 tablespoon all-purpose flour
1 teaspoon ground cumin
1 teaspoon paprika
¼ teaspoon powdered saffron *or* ½ teaspoon turmeric
¼ teaspoon ground red pepper
¼ teaspoon ground ginger
1 pound well-trimmed pork tenderloin, cut into ¾-inch medallions
1 tablespoon olive oil
1 medium onion, chopped
3 cloves garlic, minced
2½ cups chicken broth, divided
⅓ cup golden or dark raisins
1 cup uncooked couscous
¼ cup chopped fresh cilantro
¼ cup toasted sliced almonds

1. Combine flour, cumin, paprika, saffron, red pepper and ginger in medium bowl; blend well. Toss pork in flour mixture to coat.

2. Heat oil in large nonstick skillet over medium-high heat. Add onion; cook 5 minutes, stirring occasionally. Stir in garlic; add pork. Cook 4 to 5 minutes or until pork is no longer pink, turning occasionally. Add ¾ cup chicken broth and raisins; bring to a boil over high heat. Reduce heat to medium; simmer, uncovered, 7 to 8 minutes or until pork is cooked through, stirring occasionally.

3. Meanwhile, bring remaining 1¾ cups chicken broth to a boil in medium saucepan. Stir in couscous. Cover; remove from heat. Let stand 5 minutes or until liquid is absorbed.

4. Spoon couscous onto 4 plates; top with pork mixture. Sprinkle with cilantro and almonds.

Moroccan Pork Tagine

Stuffed Flank Steak

Makes 6 servings

1 cup dry red wine
¼ cup soy sauce
2 cloves garlic, minced
1 large beef flank steak (1½ to 2 pounds)
1 cup thawed frozen chopped spinach, squeezed dry
1 jar (7 ounces) roasted red bell peppers, drained and chopped
½ cup crumbled blue cheese
   Salt and black pepper

1. Combine wine, soy sauce and garlic in small bowl. Place steak in large resealable food storage bag; pour marinade over steak. Seal bag; marinate in refrigerator 2 hours.

2. Preheat oven to 350°F. Combine spinach, roasted peppers and cheese in medium bowl. Remove steak from marinade, reserving marinade. Pat steak dry and place on flat work surface.

3. Spoon spinach mixture lengthwise across two thirds of steak. Roll steak tightly around mixture, securing with toothpicks or string.

4. Season with salt and black pepper; place in roasting pan, seam side down. Bake 30 to 40 minutes for medium-rare, or until desired degree of doneness is reached, basting twice with reserved marinade. Do not baste during last 10 minutes of cooking time. Allow steak to rest about 10 minutes before slicing.

Stuffed Flank Steak

Barbecued Lamb Leg with Grilled Vegetables and Almond Pesto

Makes 6 to 8 servings

1 whole boneless leg of Australian Lamb, butterflied (see note, page 116)

Marinade
- 1 cup red wine
- ¼ cup extra-virgin olive oil
- 2 cloves of garlic, chopped
- 2 teaspoons dried oregano
- 2 teaspoons dried basil
- Freshly ground black pepper, to taste

Almond Pesto
- 1 cup chopped Italian parsley
- ½ cup chopped basil
- ⅓ cup dry roasted or blanched almonds
- ¼ cup extra-virgin olive oil
- 1 tablespoon lemon juice
- 2 tablespoons soft goat or feta cheese

Grilled Vegetables
- Halved red peppers
- Sliced eggplant
- Zucchini
- Portobella mushrooms
- Asparagus
- Olive oil, for cooking

1. Place lamb in shallow casserole dish. Combine marinade ingredients; pour over the lamb. Cover and refrigerate for 2 to 3 hours or overnight, turning lamb over once or twice. Discard marinade.

continued on page 116

Barbecued Lamb Leg with Grilled Vegetables and Almond Pesto

Barbecued Lamb Leg with Grilled Vegetables and Almond Pesto, continued

2. To make the pesto, place parsley, basil, almonds, oil and juice in food processor and process to a course paste. Add cheese and process just to combine.

3. Preheat a covered barbecue grill to medium heat. Cook lamb with hood closed turning it once or twice, about 10 to 15 minutes each side or until reaching an internal temperature of 125° to 130°F in the thickest part. Remove from grill and transfer to a plate. Cover loosely with foil and allow to rest for 10 minutes before slicing.

4. While the lamb is resting, brush the vegetables with oil and grill until lightly browned and tender. Arrange on a large platter with the sliced lamb and pesto.

Marinade Time: 2 hours or overnight • *Prep Time:* 30 minutes
Cook Time: 40 minutes

Favorite recipe from **Meat and Livestock Australia**

Note: To butterfly the lamb, remove the netting and open out the leg to make as flat as possible. Cut horizontally through the thickest portions, stopping about 1 inch from the opposite edge so that the meat can open like a book. Remove any fat thicker than ¼ inch. Lightly pound the opened meat—it should be oval in shape and have a uniform thickness.

Italian Sausage and Peppers

Makes 4 servings

3 cups (1-inch) bell pepper chunks, preferably a mix of red,
    yellow and green*
1 small onion, cut into thin wedges
3 cloves garlic, minced
4 links hot or mild Italian sausage (about 1 pound)
1 cup pasta or marinara sauce
¼ cup red wine or port
1 tablespoon cornstarch
1 tablespoon water
    Hot cooked spaghetti
¼ cup grated Parmesan or Romano cheese

Look for mixed bell pepper chunks at your supermarket salad bar.

Slow Cooker Directions

1. Coat slow cooker with cooking spray. Place bell peppers, onion and garlic in slow cooker. Arrange sausage over vegetables. Combine pasta sauce and wine; pour over sausage. Cover; cook on LOW 8 to 9 hours or on HIGH 4 to 5 hours.

2. Transfer sausage to serving platter; cover with foil to keep warm. Skim off and discard fat from juices in slow cooker.

3. Turn heat to HIGH. Mix cornstarch with water until smooth; add to slow cooker. Cook 15 minutes or until sauce is thickened, stirring once. Serve sauce over spaghetti and sausage; top with cheese.

Cook Time: 8 to 9 hours

Andalusian Lamb Kabobs

Makes 4 servings

¼ cup orange juice concentrate
2 tablespoons olive oil
2 cloves garlic, thinly sliced
1 teaspoon dried oregano
1 teaspoon ground cumin
1 teaspoon paprika
½ teaspoon salt
½ teaspoon black pepper
¼ teaspoon ground red pepper
1 pound boneless lamb leg, cut into 1-inch cubes
8 asparagus spears, diagonally cut crosswise into 2-inch pieces
2 navel oranges, cut into segments
4 cups hot cooked white or brown rice

1. For marinade, combine juice concentrate, oil, garlic, oregano, cumin, paprika, salt, black pepper and red pepper in large resealable food storage bag. Add lamb; seal bag tightly. Turn bag to coat pieces. Refrigerate at least 1 hour or up to 8 hours, turning occasionally.

2. Prepare grill for direct cooking. Alternately thread lamb, asparagus and orange sections onto skewers. Brush with marinade.

3. Grill kabobs 5 minutes on covered grill over medium-hot coals. Turn; brush with marinade. Discard remaining marinade. Grill kabobs 5 to 7 minutes more for medium or until desired doneness. Serve with rice.

Note: Andalusia is a region of southern Spain where kabobs like this are served as appetizers, but they can easily become a complete meal when accompanied by rice and a crisp green salad.

Andalusian Lamb Kabob

Tuscan Beef

Makes 4 servings

    1 tablespoon olive oil
    2 cloves garlic, minced
1½ teaspoons dried rosemary, crushed, divided
    1 teaspoon salt
    ½ teaspoon black pepper
    4 boneless beef rib eye or strip steaks (8 to 10 ounces each),
        cut ¾ to 1 inch thick
    ¾ cup prepared tomato-basil or marinara pasta sauce
    ½ cup sliced pimiento-stuffed green olives
    1 tablespoon drained capers

1. Prepare grill or preheat broiler. Combine oil, garlic, 1 teaspoon rosemary, salt and pepper in small bowl; mix well. Spread mixture evenly over both sides of steaks.

2. Place steaks on grid over medium-hot coals. Grill on covered grill, or broil 4 inches from heat source, 4 to 5 minutes per side for medium-rare (145°F internal temperature) or to desired doneness.

3. While steaks are cooking, combine pasta sauce, olives, capers and remaining ½ teaspoon rosemary in small saucepan or microwavable bowl; mix well. Heat until hot but not boiling. Transfer steaks to serving plates; top with sauce.

Tuscan Beef

Tomato-Braised Lamb Shoulder Chops with Basil-and-Olive Penne

Makes 4 to 6 servings

Tomato-Braised Chops
- 8 Australian Lamb shoulder chops, trimmed
  Salt and freshly ground pepper, to taste
- 2 tablespoons olive oil, divided
- 2 cloves garlic, chopped
- 1 onion, chopped
- 2 tablespoons tomato paste
- 1 can (about 14 ounces) crushed tomatoes
- 2 tablespoons balsamic or red wine vinegar
- ½ cup red wine
- 2 zucchini, diced

Penne
- 1 pound penne pasta
- 8 to 10 fresh basil leaves, sliced
- ¼ cup sliced black olives
- 1 to 2 tablespoons extra-virgin olive oil
  Grated Parmesan cheese, for garnish

To Serve, Optional
  Salad or vegetables of choice

1. Season lamb chops with salt and pepper. In a large deep frying pan, heat 1 tablespoon olive oil over medium-high heat. Add garlic and cook 1 minute. Add onion; cook and stir 1 to 2 minutes or until soft. Add remaining oil and lamb chops. Brown 1 to 2 minutes on each side. Add tomato paste to the pan; stir until the mixture becomes aromatic and the tomato paste changes color.

continued on page 124

Tomato-Braised Lamb Shoulder Chops with Basil-and-Olive Penne

Tomato-Braised Lamb Shoulder Chops with Basil-and-Olive Penne, continued

2. Add tomatoes with liquid, vinegar and wine; stir to combine. Bring mixture to a boil. Reduce heat to low. Cover and simmer, turning chops occasionally, about 40 to 50 minutes or until chops are very tender. Add zucchini the last 10 minutes of cooking.

3. While the lamb is cooking, prepare penne according to package directions; drain well. Fold in basil, olives and oil; mix well. Keep warm.

4. Place penne in warm bowls, top with the lamb and sprinkle with Parmesan cheese. Serve with salad or vegetables.

Prep Time: 20 minutes • **Cook Time:** 50 minutes

Favorite recipe from **Meat and Livestock Australia**

Note: When making casseroles or braised dishes, especially with lean meat such as Australian Lamb, browning the tomato paste until it turns aromatic as in this recipe adds more depth and intensity of flavor and richness.

Stuffed Eggplant

Makes 4 servings

 2 eggplants (8 to 12 ounces each)
 1 teaspoon salt
 2 tablespoons olive oil
1½ teaspoons chopped garlic
 1 teaspoon black pepper
 1 pound boneless beef sirloin steak, trimmed, cut into ¼-inch strips
 2 cups sliced red and green peppers
 2 cups sliced mushrooms
 ¼ cup water
  Pinch paprika
  Chopped fresh parsley

1. Preheat oven to 450°F. Spray baking dish with nonstick cooking spray.

2. Wash and dry eggplants. Cut off stem ends. Cut lengthwise in half; place face up in large baking dish. Pierce flat tops with fork in approximately 8 places. Sprinkle each eggplant half with ¼ teaspoon salt. Cover with foil; bake 45 minutes.

3. Meanwhile, heat oil in large nonstick skillet over medium heat. Add garlic and black pepper; cook and stir 1 to 2 minutes. Add beef; cook and stir 5 minutes.

4. Add peppers; cook 5 minutes. Add mushrooms; cook 5 minutes. Add water; stir and cover. Remove skillet from heat.

5. Remove eggplant from oven; let cool 5 minutes. Mash cooked eggplant centers with fork; do not break shells.

6. Top each half with one-fourth beef mixture; blend with cooked mashed eggplant. Cover with foil; bake 15 minutes. Remove from oven. Sprinkle with paprika and parsley.

Meaty Entrées

Baked Italian Meatballs

Makes 4 servings

  1 pound ground beef (90% to 95% lean)
  ¼ cup seasoned dry bread crumbs
  1 egg
  2 tablespoons water
  1 teaspoon minced garlic
  ½ teaspoon salt
  ⅛ teaspoon pepper
  1 jar (14½ ounces) pasta sauce, heated
    Hot cooked pasta or crusty Italian rolls (optional)

1. Heat oven to 400°F. Combine ground beef, bread crumbs, egg, water, garlic, salt and pepper in large bowl, mixing lightly but thoroughly. Shape into 12 two-inch meatballs. Place on rack in broiler pan. Bake in 400°F oven 17 to 19 minutes to medium (160°F) doneness, until not pink in center and juices show no pink color.

2. Serve with pasta sauce over hot cooked pasta or as sandwiches in crusty Italian rolls, if desired.

Prep and Cook Time: 30 to 35 minutes

Favorite recipe from **National Cattlemen's Beef Association on behalf of The Beef Checkoff**

Baked Italian Meatballs

Greek-Style Beef Kabobs

Makes 4 servings

  1 pound boneless beef sirloin steak (1 inch thick), cut into 16 pieces
¼ cup Italian salad dressing
  3 tablespoons fresh lemon juice, divided
  1 tablespoon dried oregano
  1 tablespoon Worcestershire sauce
  2 teaspoons dried basil
  1 teaspoon grated lemon peel
⅛ teaspoon red pepper flakes
  1 large green bell pepper, cut into 16 pieces
16 cherry tomatoes
  2 teaspoons olive oil
⅛ teaspoon salt

1. Combine beef, salad dressing, 2 tablespoons lemon juice, oregano, Worcestershire sauce, basil, lemon peel and red pepper flakes in large resealable food storage bag. Seal tightly; turn several times to coat. Refrigerate at least 8 hours or overnight, turning occasionally.

2. Preheat broiler. Thread 4 (10-inch) skewers with beef, alternating with bell pepper and tomatoes. Spray rimmed baking sheet or broiler pan with nonstick cooking spray. Place on baking sheet. Brush kabobs with marinade; discard remaining marinade. Broil kabobs 3 minutes. Turn over; broil 2 minutes or until desired doneness is reached. Do not overcook. Remove skewers to serving platter.

3. Add remaining 1 tablespoon lemon juice, olive oil and salt to pan drippings on baking sheet; stir well, scraping bottom of pan with flat spatula. Pour juices over kabobs.

Prep Time: 10 minutes • *Marinating Time:* 8 hours
Cook Time: 5 minutes

Greek-Style Beef Kabob

Spicy-Sweet Lamb Tagine
with Saffron Couscous

Makes 6 servings

1 tablespoon olive oil
2 pounds boneless lamb shoulder or leg, cut into 1½- to 2-inch cubes
3 medium onions, cut into eighths
3 cloves garlic, minced
2 teaspoons ground ginger
2 teaspoons ground cinnamon
1 teaspoon black pepper
2 cups water
1 can (about 14 ounces) diced tomatoes
1 can (about 15 ounces) chickpeas, rinsed and drained
1 cup chopped pitted prunes
½ teaspoon salt
1 small butternut squash, peeled and cut into 1-inch pieces
1 medium zucchini, halved and sliced crosswise into 1-inch pieces
  Saffron Couscous (page 132)
¼ cup chopped fresh cilantro or parsley

1. Heat oil in Dutch oven over high heat. Brown lamb on all sides
in 2 batches.

2. Add onions, garlic, ginger, cinnamon and pepper; stir 30 seconds
or until spices are fragrant. Add water and tomatoes. Scrape any
browned bits from bottom of pan. Cover; bring to a boil. Reduce
heat to medium-low; simmer 1 hour.

3. Remove 1 cup broth from lamb mixture; place in large saucepan.
Continue simmering lamb, covered, 30 minutes; add additional water,
if needed. Add chickpeas, prunes and salt; simmer 20 minutes or until
lamb is tender. Remove cover; simmer until broth is slightly thickened.

continued on page 132

Spicy-Sweet Lamb Tagine with Saffron Couscous

Spicy-Sweet Lamb Tagine with Saffron Couscous, continued

4. Add squash to broth in medium saucepan. Cover; bring to a boil over high heat. Reduce heat to medium-low; simmer 20 minutes or until squash is tender. Add zucchini; simmer 10 to 15 minutes or until zucchini is tender. Set aside; cover to keep warm.

5. Prepare Saffron Couscous. Place on large serving platter. Form well in center of couscous. Spoon lamb stew in center; top with vegetables. Sprinkle with cilantro.

Saffron Couscous
Makes 6 servings

    2¼ cups water
     1 tablespoon butter
     ¼ teaspoon salt
     ¼ teaspoon crushed saffron threads *or* dash powdered saffron
    10 ounces (1½ cups) uncooked couscous

1. Combine water, butter, salt and saffron in medium saucepan. Bring to a boil over high heat. Stir in couscous. Cover; remove from heat.

2. Let stand 5 minutes or until liquid is absorbed. Fluff couscous with fork.

Note: Saffron is a very expensive spice which gives food a unique flavor and tints the dish with a sunny yellow color. Saffron comes in two forms—filament-like threads and ground. Look for saffron threads which retain their flavor longer than ground saffron.

Grilled Sausage
& Tomato Pasta Toss

Makes 4 to 6 servings

8 ounces uncooked cavatappi or desired shaped pasta
1 pound sweet Italian sausage links
1 tablespoon olive oil
2 cloves garlic, minced
3 cups chopped fresh tomatoes
1 can (about 14 ounces) diced tomatoes
3 tablespoons chopped fresh basil
½ teaspoon salt
4 ounces mozzarella cheese, cubed

1. Prepare grill for direct cooking. Cook pasta according to package directions until al dente; drain and keep warm.

2. Meanwhile, grill sausage on covered grill over medium-hot coals 10 to 12 minutes or until no longer pink in center. Cut into ¼-inch slices.

3. Heat oil in large nonstick skillet over medium heat. Add garlic; cook and stir 1 minute or until golden. Add fresh tomatoes, canned tomatoes, basil and salt. Cook, stirring occasionally, 15 to 20 minutes or until tomatoes are soft and begin to fall apart.

4. Add pasta and sausage to tomato mixture; toss to coat with sauce. Add cheese; cook over low heat until cheese begins to melt.

Pesto-Crumbed Lamb Loin Chops
with Tomato-Mint Salad

Makes 4 servings

8 Australian Lamb loin chops
1 to 2 tablespoons Dijon or grainy mustard
  Olive oil, for cooking

Pesto Crumb
  ½ cup fresh bread crumbs or diced baguette
  4 large leaves fresh basil
  1 tablespoon Parmesan cheese
  1 tablespoon pine nuts, optional

Tomato-Mint Salad
  1 pint container cherry tomatoes, halved
  8 to 10 pitted green olives, sliced
  ¼ cup sliced fresh mint leaves
  1 tablespoon wine vinegar
    Salt and freshly ground pepper, to taste

1. Trim lamb chops. Brush with mustard. Place crumb ingredients
in small blender (or coffee grinder in small batches); process to combine.
Place crumbs on plate; press chops firmly onto mixture to coat both
sides. Cover with plastic and refrigerate for 10 minutes to set crumb.

2. Combine salad ingredients and set aside.

3. Heat nonstick or cast-iron pan to medium. Add enough oil to coat
base. Add chops and cook for 3 to 4 minutes on each side, or until
cooked as desired and the crust is crisp and browned.

Prep and Cook Time: 30 minutes

Favorite recipe from **Meat and Livestock Australia**

Pesto-Crumbed Lamb Loin Chops with Tomato-Mint Salad

Easy Moroccan Casserole

Makes 6 servings

2 tablespoons vegetable oil
1 pound pork stew meat, cut into 1-inch cubes
½ cup chopped onion
3 tablespoons all-purpose flour
1 can (about 14 ounces) diced tomatoes
¼ cup water
1 teaspoon ground ginger
1 teaspoon ground cumin
1 teaspoon ground cinnamon
½ teaspoon sugar
½ teaspoon salt
½ teaspoon black pepper
2 medium unpeeled red potatoes, cut into ½-inch pieces
1 large sweet potato, peeled and cut into ½-inch pieces
1 cup frozen lima beans, thawed and drained
1 cup frozen cut green beans, thawed and drained
¾ cup sliced carrots
Pita bread

1. Preheat oven to 325°F.

2. Heat oil in large skillet over medium-high heat. Add pork and onion; brown pork on all sides. Sprinkle flour over meat mixture. Stir until flour has absorbed pan juices. Cook 2 minutes more.

3. Stir in tomatoes, water, ginger, cumin, cinnamon, sugar, salt and pepper. Transfer mixture to 2-quart casserole. Bake 30 minutes.

4. Add red potatoes, sweet potato, lima beans, green beans and carrots; mix well. Cover; bake 1 hour or until potatoes are tender. Serve with pita bread.

Easy Moroccan Casserole

Spanish Beef Stew

Makes 6 to 8 servings

4 tablespoons olive oil, divided
1 medium onion, chopped
3 cloves garlic, chopped
2 pounds boneless beef chuck roast, trimmed and cut into ½-inch pieces
 or 2 pounds beef for stew
1 can (28 ounces) whole peeled tomatoes, undrained, coarsely chopped
2 sweet potatoes, peeled, quartered and sliced (about 1 pound)
1 can (10½ ounces) condensed beef broth
1 medium green bell pepper, cut into pieces
1 cup frozen corn
3 tablespoons balsamic or red wine vinegar
½ teaspoon dried coriander *or* 1½ teaspoons finely chopped fresh cilantro*
¼ teaspoon ground red pepper *or* ½ teaspoon red pepper flakes
2 tablespoons water
2 tablespoons cornstarch
 Hot cooked rice
 Chopped fresh cilantro (optional)

When using fresh cilantro, add to stew last 5 minutes of cooking.

1. Heat 1 tablespoon oil in 5-quart Dutch oven over medium-high heat. Cook and stir onion and garlic until onion is soft. Remove with slotted spoon; set aside.

2. Add 2 tablespoons oil to Dutch oven. Brown half of beef over medium-high heat. Remove with slotted spoon; set aside. Brown remaining beef in remaining 1 tablespoon oil. Pour off drippings. Return beef, onion and garlic to Dutch oven.

3. Add tomatoes with juice, sweet potatoes, broth, bell pepper, corn, vinegar, coriander and red pepper. Bring to a boil over high heat. Reduce heat to low. Cover; simmer 40 minutes.

4. Blend water into cornstarch in small cup until smooth. Stir into stew. Cook and stir until stew boils and sauce is slightly thickened. Serve with rice. Garnish with cilantro.

Moroccan-Seasoned Chops
with Fruited Couscous

Makes 4 servings

  4 boneless pork chops, ¾ inch thick
 ¾ teaspoon ground cumin
 ¾ teaspoon ground coriander
 ⅛ teaspoon ground cinnamon
 ⅛ teaspoon cayenne (ground red pepper)
  1 teaspoon olive oil
  1 cup uncooked couscous
 ¼ cup raisins
 ¼ cup chopped dried apricots
  1 tablespoon pine nuts
    Cooking oil spray

In small bowl combine cumin, coriander, cinnamon and cayenne; rub mixture onto both sides of pork chops. Heat oil in large nonstick skillet over medium-high heat; cook chops, turning once, about 6 to 8 minutes.

Meanwhile, prepare couscous according to label directions, adding raisins, apricots and pine nuts to cooking water.

Serve chops on top of couscous.

Favorite recipe from **National Pork Board**

Greek Lamb Burgers

Makes 4 servings

¼ cup pine nuts
1 pound ground lamb
¼ cup finely chopped yellow onion
3 cloves garlic, minced, divided
¾ teaspoon salt
¼ teaspoon black pepper
¼ cup plain yogurt
¼ teaspoon sugar
4 slices red onion (¼ inch thick)
1 tablespoon olive oil
8 pumpernickel bread slices
12 thin cucumber slices
4 tomato slices

1. Prepare grill for direct cooking. Meanwhile, heat small skillet over medium heat. Add pine nuts; cook 30 to 45 seconds until light brown, shaking pan occasionally.

2. Combine lamb, pine nuts, yellow onion, 2 cloves garlic, salt and pepper in large bowl; mix well. Shape mixture into 4 patties, about ½ inch thick and 4 inches in diameter. Combine yogurt, sugar and remaining 1 clove garlic in small bowl; set aside.

3. Brush 1 side of each patty and red onion slice with oil; place on grid, oiled sides down. Brush tops with oil. Grill on covered grill over medium-hot coals 8 to 10 minutes for medium or to desired doneness, turning halfway through grilling time. Place bread on grid to toast during last few minutes of grilling time; grill 1 to 2 minutes per side.

4. Top 4 bread slices with patties and red onion slices; top each with 3 cucumber slices and 1 tomato slice. Dollop evenly with yogurt mixture. Top sandwiches with remaining 4 bread slices.

Greek Lamb Burger

Poultry

Spanish Braised Chicken with Green Olives and Rice

Makes 6 servings

2 pounds bone-in skinless chicken thighs
1 teaspoon paprika
1 tablespoon olive oil
¾ cup dry sherry
2¼ cups water
1 can (about 14 ounces) chicken broth
¾ cup sliced pimiento-stuffed green olives
1½ teaspoons dried sage
1½ cups uncooked long-grain white rice

1. Sprinkle chicken thighs with paprika. Heat oil in large skillet over medium-high heat. Brown chicken 3 to 4 minutes on each side or until golden.

2. Remove chicken from skillet. Add sherry stirring to scrape up bits from bottom of skillet. Add water, chicken broth, olives and sage; bring to a boil. Reduce heat to low. Return chicken to skillet. Cover; simmer 10 minutes.

3. Add rice to liquid around chicken; gently stir to distribute evenly in skillet. Cover; simmer 20 to 25 minutes or until liquid is absorbed and rice is tender.

Poultry

Chicken Cassoulet
Makes 6 servings

4 slices bacon
¼ cup all-purpose flour
   Salt and black pepper
1¾ pounds bone-in chicken pieces
2 cooked chicken sausages, cut into ¼-inch pieces
1 onion, chopped
1½ cups diced red and green bell peppers (2 small bell peppers)
2 cloves garlic, finely chopped
1 teaspoon dried thyme
   Salt and black pepper
   Olive oil
2 cans (about 15 ounces each) cannellini or Great Northern beans,
   rinsed and drained
½ cup dry white wine (optional)

1. Preheat oven to 350°F. Cook bacon in large skillet over medium-high heat until crisp. Drain on paper towels. Crumble into 1-inch pieces.

2. Pour off all but 2 tablespoons fat from skillet. Place flour in shallow bowl; season with salt and black pepper. Dip chicken pieces in flour mixture; shake off excess. Brown chicken in batches over medium-high heat in skillet; remove and set aside. Lightly brown sausages in same skillet; remove and set aside.

3. Add onion, bell peppers, garlic, thyme, salt and black pepper to skillet. Cook and stir over medium heat about 5 minutes or until softened, adding olive oil as needed to prevent sticking. Transfer onion mixture to 13×9-inch baking dish. Add beans; mix well. Top with chicken, sausages and bacon. Add wine to skillet, if desired; cook and stir over medium heat, scraping up brown bits on bottom of pan. Pour over casserole.

4. Cover; bake 40 minutes. Uncover; bake 15 minutes more or until chicken is cooked through (180°F).

Chicken Cassoulet

Mediterranean Chicken Kabobs

Makes 8 servings

2 pounds boneless skinless chicken breasts or chicken tenders,
    cut into 1-inch pieces
1 small eggplant, peeled and cut into 1-inch pieces
1 medium zucchini, cut crosswise into ½-inch slices
2 medium onions, each cut into 8 wedges
16 medium mushrooms, stems removed
16 cherry tomatoes
1 cup chicken broth
⅔ cup balsamic vinegar
3 tablespoons olive oil
2 tablespoons dried mint
4 teaspoons dried basil
1 tablespoon dried oregano
2 teaspoons grated lemon peel
    Chopped fresh parsley
4 cups hot cooked couscous

1. Alternately thread chicken, eggplant, zucchini, onions, mushrooms
and tomatoes onto 16 metal skewers; place in large glass baking dish.

2. Combine chicken broth, vinegar, oil, mint, basil and oregano in small
bowl; pour over kabobs. Cover; marinate in refrigerator 2 hours, turning
kabobs occasionally. Remove kabobs from marinade; discard marinade.

3. Preheat broiler. Broil kabobs 6 inches from heat 10 to 15 minutes or
until chicken is cooked through, turning kabobs halfway through
cooking time.

4. Stir lemon peel and parsley into couscous; serve with kabobs.

Poultry

Tip: These kabobs can be grilled instead of broiled. Spray the grill grid with nonstick cooking spray; then prepare grill for direct grilling. Grill the kabobs on a covered grill over medium-hot coals 10 to 15 minutes or until the chicken is cooked through. Turn the kabobs halfway through the cooking time.

Mediterranean Chicken Kabobs

Mediterranean Chicken with Dried Fruits & Olives

Makes 4 servings

     4 boneless, skinless chicken breast halves (about 1¼ pounds)
 1½ teaspoons ground cumin
   ½ teaspoon salt
   ¼ teaspoon ground black pepper
   ¼ cup I CAN'T BELIEVE IT'S NOT BUTTER!® Spread
     4 cloves garlic, finely chopped
 1½ cups mixed dried fruits
     1 cup dry white wine or chicken broth
     1 cup chicken broth
   ½ cup pimiento-stuffed olives, sliced

Season chicken with cumin, salt and pepper. In 12-inch skillet, melt I Can't Believe It's Not Butter!® Spread over medium-high heat and brown chicken. Add garlic and cook 30 seconds. Stir in dried fruits, wine, broth and olives. Bring just to a boil. Reduce heat to low and simmer uncovered, stirring occasionally, 10 minutes or until chicken is thoroughly cooked. Remove chicken to serving platter and keep warm.

Bring sauce to a boil over high heat and continue boiling, stirring occasionally, 6 minutes or until sauce is slightly thickened. To serve, spoon fruit sauce over chicken.

Note: Recipe can be halved.

Poultry

Lemon-Mint Meatballs
with Lemon Orzo

Makes 3 to 4 servings

12 ounces ground chicken
2 green onions, minced
2 tablespoons minced fresh mint
1 egg *or* 2 tablespoons cholesterol-free egg substitute
3 teaspoons grated lemon peel, divided
6 cloves garlic, divided
½ teaspoon dried oregano
¼ teaspoon black pepper
3 cups chicken broth
1 cup (6 ounces) uncooked orzo pasta
1 tablespoon lemon juice
½ (10-ounce) package fresh spinach leaves, washed and torn

1. Spray 11×7-inch microwavable baking dish with nonstick cooking spray. Combine chicken, green onions, mint, egg, 2 teaspoons lemon peel, 3 minced cloves garlic, oregano and pepper in medium bowl; mix until well blended. Shape into 12 meatballs and place in baking dish, spacing evenly apart.

2. Slice remaining 3 cloves garlic; place in large saucepan. Add chicken broth; bring to a boil over high heat. Stir in orzo. Reduce heat to medium; simmer 8 to 10 minutes or until tender. Reduce heat to low; stir in remaining 1 teaspoon lemon peel and lemon juice. Stir in spinach, 1 handful at a time, until incorporated. Stir until spinach is wilted. Remove from heat; cover to keep warm.

3. Place meatballs in microwave. Microwave on HIGH 2 minutes. Rearrange meatballs, moving them from outer edges to center of dish. Microwave on HIGH 1 to 2 minutes more or until cooked through (160°F). Spoon orzo into wide bowls or rimmed plates. Top with meatballs.

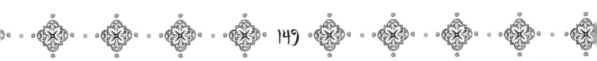

Poultry

Roasted Chicken & Garlic Provençale

Makes 4 servings

1 envelope LIPTON® RECIPE SECRETS® Savory Herb with
   Garlic Soup Mix
3 tablespoons BERTOLLI® Olive Oil
2 tablespoons water
1 tablespoon white wine vinegar (optional)
1 (2½- to 3-pound) chicken, cut into serving pieces
1 large onion, cut into 8 wedges
1 large tomato, cut into 8 wedges

1. Preheat oven to 425°F. In small bowl, combine soup mix, olive oil, water and vinegar.

2. In broiler pan, without the rack, arrange chicken, onion and tomato. Pour soup mixture over chicken and vegetables.

3. Roast 45 minutes or until chicken is thoroughly cooked.

Note: Recipes prepared in the style of Provence, a region in southeastern France, are typically prepared with garlic, tomatoes and olive oil. Other ingredients common to this region include onions, olives, mushrooms, anchovies and eggplant.

Roasted Chicken & Garlic Provençale

Pesto-Coated Baked Chicken

Makes 4 servings

1 pound boneless skinless chicken breasts, cut into ½-inch-thick cutlets
¼ cup plus 1 tablespoon prepared pesto
1½ teaspoons sour cream
1½ teaspoons mayonnaise
1 tablespoon shredded Parmesan cheese
1 tablespoon pine nuts

1. Preheat oven to 450°F. Arrange chicken in single layer in shallow baking pan. Combine pesto, sour cream and mayonnaise in small cup. Brush over chicken. Sprinkle with cheese and pine nuts.

2. Bake 8 to 10 minutes or until chicken is no longer pink in center.

Variation: Chicken can be cooked on an oiled grid over a preheated grill.

Chicken Pomodoro
with Tomato Basil Garlic

Makes 8 servings

4 teaspoons olive oil
8 boneless skinless chicken breast halves
8 ounces fresh mushrooms, sliced
2 cans (14¼ ounces each) Italian-style stewed tomatoes
8 teaspoons MRS. DASH® Tomato Basil Garlic Seasoning
½ cup semi-dry white wine (optional)

Heat oil in nonstick skillet. Add chicken and brown over medium heat about 10 minutes, turning once. Add remaining ingredients. Bring to a boil; reduce heat and simmer, uncovered, 15 minutes.

Prep Time: 10 minutes • *Cook Time:* 25 minutes

Pesto-Coated Baked Chicken

Moroccan Chicken, Apricot & Almond Casserole

Makes 4 to 6 servings

1 pound ground chicken*
¾ teaspoon salt, divided
¼ teaspoon ground cinnamon
¼ teaspoon black pepper
1 tablespoon olive oil
1 small onion, chopped
1 cup sliced dried apricots
1 can (28 ounces) diced tomatoes
½ teaspoon red pepper flakes
½ teaspoon ground ginger
1 can (10½ ounces) condensed chicken broth
½ cup water
1 cup large-pearl couscous**
¼ cup toasted sliced almonds

Ground turkey or lamb can be substituted for the ground chicken.

**Large-pearl couscous, which is the size of barley, is available in many supermarkets. If it is not available, substitute regular small-grain couscous.*

1. Preheat oven to 325°F.

2. Combine chicken, ½ teaspoon salt, cinnamon and black pepper in medium bowl. Shape into 1-inch balls. Heat oil in large skillet. Add meatballs; brown on all sides. Remove to plate. Add onion and apricots to skillet. Cook 5 minutes over medium heat or until onion is tender. Stir in tomatoes, remaining ¼ teaspoon salt, red pepper flakes and ginger. Simmer 5 minutes.

3. Meanwhile, bring chicken broth and water to a boil in small saucepan. Stir in large pearl couscous.*** Reduce heat. Cover; simmer 10 minutes or until couscous is tender and almost all liquid has been absorbed. Drain if necessary.

4. Spoon couscous into greased 11×7-inch casserole dish. Top with meatballs; spoon tomato mixture over meatballs. Bake in preheated oven 20 minutes or until chicken is cooked through (165°F). Sprinkle with almonds.

***To cook small-grain couscous, follow package directions using 1 cup chicken broth in place of water. Remove from heat and let stand 5 minutes or until all liquid is absorbed. Fluff with a fork.

Moroccan Chicken, Apricot & Almond Casserole

Middle Eastern Grilled Chicken Kebabs

Makes 4 servings

　1 pound skinless, boneless chicken breasts, cut into 1 inch pieces
16 cherry tomatoes
　8 (6-inch) skewers

Marinade
　1 cup plain yogurt
　1 tablespoon chopped fresh mint
　3 cloves garlic, minced
　½ teaspoon salt

Salad
　1 large tomato, chopped
　1 medium cucumber (peeled if waxed), chopped
½ small red onion, diced
　2 teaspoons chopped fresh parsley
　2 cloves garlic, minced
　2 tablespoons extra-virgin olive oil
　2 tablespoons red wine vinegar
　　Salt and pepper to taste
　　Kalamata olives to garnish
　　Fresh mint sprigs to garnish

Pita Bread
　4 rounds pita bread
　2 tablespoons extra-virgin olive oil
　2 cloves garlic, minced

Whisk together the marinade ingredients in medium bowl. Add chicken pieces, mixing until well-coated with marinade. Cover and refrigerate for 1 hour.

Poultry

Prepare grill for direct cooking.

To make salad, toss all salad ingredients together in a medium bowl. Cover and set aside to let the flavors blend.

To prepare pitas, stir together olive oil and garlic in a small bowl or cup. Brush oil mixture on both sides of pitas; set aside until you are ready to grill.

Thread chicken pieces and cherry tomatoes onto the skewers. Grill kebabs over hot coals 8 minutes or until kebabs are well-charred and very firm to the touch. Just before the chicken is done, grill both sides of pitas until lightly browned.

To serve, cut pitas into triangles and arrange on each of 4 plates. Spoon salad onto each plate and set kebabs on top of each salad. Garnish with olives and fresh mint sprigs.

Favorite recipe from **National Chicken Council**

Poultry

Paella
Makes 4 to 6 servings

¼ cup FILIPPO BERIO® Olive Oil
1 pound boneless skinless chicken breasts, cut into 1-inch strips
½ pound Italian sausage links, cut into 1-inch slices
1 onion, chopped
3 cloves garlic, minced
2 (14½-ounce) cans chicken broth
2 cups uncooked long grain white rice
1 (8-ounce) bottle clam juice
1 (2-ounce) jar chopped pimientos, drained
2 bay leaves
1 teaspoon salt
¼ teaspoon saffron threads, crumbled (optional)
1 pound raw shrimp, shelled and deveined
1 (16-ounce) can whole tomatoes, drained
1 (10-ounce) package frozen peas, thawed
12 littleneck clams, scrubbed
¼ cup water

Preheat oven to 350°F. In large skillet, heat olive oil over medium heat. Add chicken; cook and stir 8 to 10 minutes or until brown on all sides. Remove with slotted spoon; set aside. Add sausage to skillet; cook and stir 8 to 10 minutes or until brown. Remove with slotted spoon; set aside. Add onion and garlic to skillet; cook and stir 5 to 7 minutes or until onion is tender. Transfer chicken, sausage, onion and garlic mixture to large casserole.

Add chicken broth, rice, clam juice, pimientos, bay leaves, salt and saffron, if desired, to chicken mixture. Cover; bake 30 minutes. Add shrimp, tomatoes and peas; stir well. Cover; bake an additional 15 minutes or until rice is tender, liquid is absorbed and shrimp are opaque. Remove bay leaves.

Meanwhile, combine clams and water in stockpot or large saucepan. Cover; cook over medium heat 5 to 10 minutes or until clams open; remove clams immediately as they open. Discard any clams with unopened shells. Place clams on top of paella.

Paella

Cornish Hens with New Potatoes, Artichokes and Peas

Makes 4 servings

4 PERDUE® Fresh Cornish Hens, wings tucked under, legs tied together
3 lemons, halved
¼ cup fresh basil, chopped
2 tablespoons olive oil
  Salt and pepper
1 pound new potatoes, halved or quartered if large
2 (14-ounce) cans artichoke hearts in water, drained and halved
1 cup chicken broth
1 cup frozen peas, thawed

Preheat oven to 350°F. Set Cornish hens in a large roasting pan and squeeze lemons over them. Sprinkle with basil, olive oil, salt and pepper. Scatter potatoes and artichoke hearts around Cornish hens and add chicken broth. Season vegetables with salt and pepper. Roast until meat thermometer inserted into thickest part of thigh registers 165°F (approximately 1 hour).

Transfer Cornish hens to a serving platter. Stir peas into vegetables and transfer to a serving dish.

Prep Time: 20 minutes • *Cook Time:* 1 hour

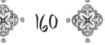

Chicken Prosciutto Rolls

Makes 4 servings

1 can (28 ounces) tomato sauce
2 cloves garlic, minced
1 teaspoon dried oregano
1 teaspoon dried basil
4 boneless skinless chicken breasts
8 slices prosciutto
1 jar (12 ounces) roasted red peppers, drained and cut in half
1 cup grated Asiago cheese, divided
   Hot cooked spaghetti

1. Preheat oven to 350°F. Combine tomato sauce, garlic, oregano
and basil in medium bowl. Spoon 1 cup sauce onto bottom of 3-quart
covered casserole; set aside. Reserve remaining sauce.

2. Slice each chicken breast in half crosswise to make 8 thin pieces.
Using meat mallet, pound each piece to ¼-inch thickness.

3. Place prosciutto slice (fold in half to fit), 1 roasted pepper half and
1 tablespoon cheese on each piece of chicken. Roll up chicken with
filling starting from longer side. Place rolls seam sides down in prepared
casserole. Pour reserved sauce over chicken.

4. Cover and bake 50 minutes or until chicken in no longer pink
in center. Sprinkle with remaining ½ cup cheese. Bake, uncovered,
10 minutes or until cheese is melted. Slice chicken rolls; serve with
sauce over spaghetti.

Lemon-Dijon Chicken with Potatoes

Makes 6 servings

  2 medium lemons
½ cup chopped fresh parsley
  2 tablespoons Dijon mustard
  4 cloves garlic, minced
  2 teaspoons olive oil
  1 teaspoon dried rosemary
¾ teaspoon black pepper
½ teaspoon salt
  1 whole chicken (about 3½ pounds)
1½ pounds small red potatoes, cut into halves

1. Preheat oven to 350°F.

2. Squeeze 3 tablespoons juice from lemons; reserve squeezed lemon halves. Combine parsley, lemon juice, mustard, garlic, oil, rosemary, pepper and salt in small bowl; blend well. Reserve 2 tablespoons mixture.

3. Place chicken on rack in baking pan. Gently slide fingers between skin and meat of chicken breasts and drumsticks to separate skin from meat, being careful not to tear skin. Spoon parsley mixture between skin and meat. (Secure breast skin with toothpicks, if necessary.) Discard any remaining parsley mixture. Place lemon halves in cavity of chicken. Bake 30 minutes.

4. Meanwhile, toss potatoes with reserved parsley mixture until coated. Arrange potatoes around chicken; bake 1 hour or until juices in chicken run clear and thermometer inserted in thickest part of thigh registers 180°F. Remove chicken from oven; let stand 10 minutes. Remove skin; slice chicken. Sprinkle any accumulated parsley mixture from pan over chicken and potatoes.

Lemon-Dijon Chicken with Potatoes

Braised Chicken Thighs
with Fruited Rice and Lentils

Makes 6 servings

        1 tablespoon olive oil
        6 chicken thighs
   3½ cups canned chicken broth
    ¾ cup uncooked basmati rice
        1 medium onion, chopped
        2 tablespoons balsamic vinegar
        2 teaspoons sugar
        1 teaspoon ground cumin
        1 teaspoon ground cinnamon
    ¼ teaspoon black pepper
        1 cup uncooked red lentils
    ⅔ cup quartered dried apricots
    ½ cup raisins
    ¼ cup chopped fresh cilantro or parsley

1. Heat oil in Dutch oven over medium-high heat. Add chicken; cook 10 minutes or until browned, turning once. Remove chicken; set aside.

2. Add chicken broth, rice, onion, vinegar, sugar, cumin, cinnamon and pepper to saucepan; bring to a boil over high heat. Reduce heat to low; simmer, covered, 15 minutes. Stir in lentils, apricots and raisins.

3. Arrange chicken on top of rice mixture in saucepan. Cover; simmer 40 to 45 minutes until liquid is absorbed and rice and lentils are tender.

4. Transfer chicken to serving platter. Stir cilantro into rice mixture. Spoon rice mixture around chicken.

    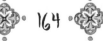

Braised Chicken Thighs with Fruited Rice and Lentils

Portuguese Chicken
with Peppers and Olives

Makes 6 servings

6 boneless skinless chicken breasts
1 teaspoon salt
½ teaspoon red pepper flakes
¼ teaspoon black pepper
3 tablespoons olive oil, divided
2 large onions, halved and sliced
2 red bell peppers, sliced
2 cloves garlic, minced
½ cup sliced black olives

1. Preheat oven to 475°F. Sprinkle chicken with salt, pepper flakes and black pepper. Heat 1 tablespoon oil in large nonstick skillet over medium-high heat. Add chicken; cook 3 to 4 minutes. Turn chicken; cook 4 minutes more. Remove chicken to casserole with cover.

2. Heat remaining 2 tablespoons oil in same skillet. Add onions; cook and stir 2 to 3 minutes or until softened. Add bell peppers and garlic; cook, covered, 2 to 3 minutes longer. Stir in olives.

3. Pour onion mixture over chicken. Cover; bake 15 minutes or until chicken is no longer pink in center.

Prep Time: 5 minutes • ***Cook Time:*** 25 minutes

Poultry

Handkerchief Pasta
with Chicken and Chard

Makes 4 servings

2 bunches chard (to make 9 cups chopped, loosely packed)
1 package (about 8 ounces) flat lasagna noodles
4 tablespoons extra-virgin olive oil, divided
3 cloves garlic, minced
2 boneless skinless chicken breasts, cut into bite-size pieces
    Salt and pepper
¼ cup balsamic vinegar
    Toasted pine nuts

1. Trim chard; pull leaves from large stems. Chop stems; roll leaves into bundles and slice into ribbons.

2. Bring large saucepan of salted water to a boil. Break lasagna noodles into halves or thirds to made square handkerchief-shaped pasta. (Don't worry if some pieces break unevenly.) Cook pasta in boiling water until tender but firm. Drain; oil lightly to prevent sticking. Keep warm.

3. Heat 2 tablespoons oil in large skillet or Dutch oven over medium heat. Add garlic; cook and stir 30 seconds. Add chicken; cook and stir about 2 minutes. Add remaining 2 tablespoons oil; mix in chard. Season with salt and pepper. Cover and cook until chard is wilted, stirring occasionally. Stir balsamic vinegar into skillet. Cook 3 to 5 minutes or until chicken is cooked through and flavors are blended.

4. Arrange 3 or 4 pieces of pasta on each serving plate. Top with chicken mixture; sprinkle with pine nuts.

Vegetables & More

Peperonata
Makes 4 to 5 servings

1 tablespoon extra-virgin olive oil
4 large red, yellow or orange bell peppers, cut into thin strips
2 cloves garlic, coarsely chopped
12 pimiento-stuffed green olives or pitted black olives, sliced or chopped
2 to 3 tablespoons white wine or red wine vinegar
¼ teaspoon salt
¼ teaspoon black pepper

1. Heat olive oil in 12-inch skillet over medium-high heat. Add bell peppers; cook 8 or 9 minutes, stirring frequently until edges of peppers begin to brown.

2. Reduce heat to medium. Add garlic; cook and stir 1 to 2 minutes. *Do not allow garlic to brown.* Add olives, vinegar, salt and black pepper. Cook 1 to 2 minutes or until all liquid has evaporated.

Note: Traditionally, peperonata is served hot as a condiment with meat dishes. Or, it can be chilled and served as part of an antipasti selection. It also makes a great side dish which complements both chicken and pork.

Gemelli & Grilled Summer Vegetables

Makes 4 (1½-cup) servings

  2 large bell peppers (red and yellow)
 12 stalks asparagus
  2 slices red onion
  3 tablespoons plus 1 teaspoon extra-virgin olive oil, divided
  6 ounces (2¼ cups) gemelli or rotini pasta
  2 tablespoons pine nuts
  1 clove garlic
  1 cup loosely packed basil leaves
  ¼ cup grated Parmesan cheese
  ¼ teaspoon salt
  ¼ teaspoon black pepper
  1 cup grape or cherry tomatoes

1. Prepare grill for direct cooking. Cut bell peppers in half; remove and discard seeds. Place asparagus and onion on large plate; coat with 1 teaspoon olive oil.

2. Grill bell peppers, skin side down, on covered grill over medium heat 10 to 12 minutes or until skins are blackened. Place peppers in paper or plastic bag; let stand 15 minutes. Remove and discard blackened skin. Cut peppers into chunks.

3. Cook pasta according to package directions; drain and return to pan. Meanwhile, grill asparagus and onion on covered grill over medium heat 8 to 10 minutes or until tender, turning once. Cut asparagus into 2-inch pieces; cut onion into small pieces. Add vegetables to pasta.

4. Place pine nuts and garlic in food processor. Process until coarsely chopped. Add basil; process until finely chopped. While processor is running, add remaining 3 tablespoons olive oil until mixture is blended. Stir in cheese, salt and pepper. Add basil mixture and tomatoes to pasta; toss until pasta is coated. Serve immediately.

Gemelli & Grilled Summer Vegetables

Smoky Kale Chiffonade

Makes 4 side-dish servings

¾ pound fresh young kale or mustard greens
3 slices bacon
2 tablespoons crumbled blue cheese

1. Rinse kale well in large bowl of warm water; place in colander. Drain. Discard any discolored leaves; trim away tough stem ends. To prepare chiffonade, roll up leaves jelly-roll fashion. Slice crosswise into ½-inch slices; separate into strips. Set aside.

2. Cook bacon in medium skillet over medium heat until crisp. Remove bacon to paper towel. Remove all but 1 tablespoon drippings.

3. Add kale to drippings in skillet. Cook and stir over medium-high heat 2 to 3 minutes until wilted and tender (older leaves may take slightly longer).*

4. Crumble bacon. Toss bacon and blue cheese with kale. Transfer to warm serving dish. Serve immediately.

*If using mustard greens, cook 4 to 6 minutes until wilted and tender.

Note: *"Chiffonade" in French literally means "made of rags." In cooking, it means "cut into thin strips."*

Smoky Kale Chiffonade

Asparagus-Parmesan Risotto

Makes 4 to 5 main-dish servings

5½ cups chicken broth
⅛ teaspoon salt
4 tablespoons unsalted butter, divided
⅓ cup finely chopped onion
2 cups arborio rice
⅔ cup dry white wine
2½ cups fresh asparagus pieces (about 1 inch long)
⅔ cup frozen peas
1 cup grated Parmesan cheese

1. Bring broth and salt to a boil in medium saucepan over medium-high heat; reduce heat to low and simmer.

2. Meanwhile, melt 3 tablespoons butter in large saucepan over medium heat. Add onion; cook and stir 2 to 3 minutes or until tender. Stir in rice; cook, stirring frequently 2 minutes or until most of rice grains are opaque. Add wine; cook, stirring occasionally until most of wine evaporates.

3. Add 1½ cups broth; cook and stir 6 to 7 minutes or until most of liquid has been absorbed. (Mixture should simmer, but not boil.) Add 2 cups broth and asparagus; cook and stir 6 to 7 minutes until most of liquid has been absorbed. Add remaining 2 cups broth and peas; cook and stir 5 to 6 minutes or until most of liquid has been absorbed and rice mixture is creamy.

4. Remove from heat; stir in remaining 1 tablespoon butter and cheese until melted. Season to taste with salt.

Tip: Broth can be added in smaller increments of ½ to ¾ cup, if desired. Just be sure to stir the rice mixture constantly for a creamy texture.

continued on page 176

Asparagus-Parmesan Risotto

Asparagus-Parmesan Risotto, continued

Asparagus-Spinach Risotto: Substitute 1 cup fresh baby spinach leaves or chopped large spinach leaves for peas. Add the spinach at the end of step 3; cover and let stand 1 minute or until spinach is wilted. Proceed with step 4.

Asparagus-Chicken Risotto: Add 2 cups chopped or shredded cooked chicken to risotto with peas in step 3. Proceed as directed.

Sautéed Swiss Chard

Makes 4 (½-cup) servings

1 large bunch Swiss chard or kale (about 1 pound)
1 tablespoon olive oil
3 cloves garlic, minced
¾ teaspoon salt
¼ teaspoon black pepper
1 tablespoon balsamic vinegar
¼ cup pine nuts, toasted

1. Rinse chard in cold water; shake off excess water but do not dry. Finely chop stems and coarsely chop leaves.

2. Heat oil in large saucepan or Dutch oven over medium heat. Add garlic; cook and stir 2 minutes. Add chard, salt and pepper. Cover and steam for 2 minutes or until chard begins to wilt. Uncover; cook and stir about 5 minutes until chard is evenly wilted.

3. Stir in vinegar; sprinkle with pine nuts before serving.

Vegetables & More

Tabbouleh
Makes 8 servings

½ cup uncooked bulgur wheat
¾ cup boiling water
¼ teaspoon salt
5 teaspoons lemon juice
2 teaspoons olive oil
½ teaspoon dried basil
¼ teaspoon black pepper
1 green onion, thinly sliced
½ cup chopped cucumber
½ cup chopped green bell pepper
½ cup chopped tomato
¼ cup chopped fresh parsley
2 teaspoons chopped fresh mint

1. Rinse bulgur thoroughly in colander under cold water, picking out any debris; drain well. Transfer to medium heatproof bowl. Stir in boiling water and salt. Cover; let stand 30 minutes. Drain well.

2. Combine lemon juice, oil, basil and black pepper in small bowl. Pour over bulgur; mix well.

3. Layer bulgur, green onion, cucumber, bell pepper and tomato in clear glass bowl; sprinkle with parsley and mint.

4. Refrigerate, covered, at least 2 hours to allow flavors to blend. Serve layered or toss before serving.

Vegetables & More

Mediterranean Stew
Makes 6 servings

   8 ounces fresh okra *or* 1 package (10 ounces) frozen cut okra
   1 tablespoon olive oil
1½ cups chopped onion
   1 clove garlic, minced
   ½ teaspoon ground cumin
   ½ teaspoon ground turmeric
   ¼ teaspoon ground cinnamon
   ¼ teaspoon ground red pepper
   ¼ teaspoon paprika
   1 medium butternut or acorn squash, peeled and cut into 1-inch cubes
   2 cups unpeeled eggplant, cut into 1-inch cubes
   2 cups sliced zucchini
   1 medium carrot, thinly sliced
   1 can (8 ounces) tomato sauce
   ½ cup vegetable broth
   1 can (about 15 ounces) chickpeas, rinsed and drained
   1 medium tomato, chopped
   ⅓ cup raisins
      Salt
   6 to 8 cups hot cooked couscous or rice

1. Wash okra under cold running water. Cut into ¾-inch slices. Heat
oil in large saucepan over high heat. Add onion and garlic; cook and stir
5 minutes or until tender. Stir in cumin, turmeric, cinnamon, red pepper
and paprika; cook and stir 2 to 3 minutes.

2. Add okra, squash, eggplant, zucchini, carrot, tomato sauce and broth.
Bring to a boil over high heat. Reduce heat to low. simmer, uncovered,
5 minutes.

3. Add chickpeas, tomato and raisins; simmer, covered, 30 minutes.
Season with salt. Serve over couscous. Garnish with parsley.

Mediterranean Stew

Spanish Paella-Style Rice

Makes 6 servings

2 cans (about 14 ounces each) chicken broth
1½ cups uncooked converted long-grain rice
1 small red bell pepper, diced
⅓ cup dry white wine or water
½ teaspoon crushed saffron threads *or* ½ teaspoon ground turmeric
⅛ teaspoon red pepper flakes
½ cup frozen peas, thawed
Salt

Slow Cooker Directions
1. Combine broth, rice, bell pepper, wine, saffron and red pepper flakes in 2½-quart slow cooker; mix well. Cover; cook on LOW 4 hours or until liquid is absorbed.

2. Stir in peas. Cover; cook 15 to 30 minutes or until peas are hot. Season with salt.

Prep Time: 10 minutes • *Cook Time:* 4½ hours

Variation: Add ½ cup cooked chicken, ham or shrimp with the peas.

Note: Paella is a traditional Spanish dish made with saffron-flavored rice and typically combined with a variety of meats, seafood and vegetables. Since saffron is expensive, turmeric is sometimes given as an alternative. While the finished dish looks similar, the flavor is different.

Spanish Paella-Style Rice

Eggplant Italiano

Makes 6 servings

2 tablespoons olive oil, divided
2 medium onions, halved and thinly sliced
2 stalks celery, cut into 1-inch pieces
1¼ pounds eggplant, cut into 1-inch cubes
1 can (about 14 ounces) diced tomatoes, drained
½ cup pitted black olives, cut crosswise in half
2 tablespoons balsamic vinegar
1 tablespoon sugar
1 tablespoon drained capers
1 teaspoon dried oregano or basil
Salt and black pepper

1. Heat 1 tablespoon oil in large skillet over medium-high heat. Add onions and celery; cook and stir about 2 minutes or until tender. Move onions and celery to side of skillet. Reduce heat to medium.

2. Add remaining 1 tablespoon oil; heat 30 seconds. Add eggplant; cook and stir about 4 minutes or until tender. Add tomatoes; mix well. Cover; cook 10 minutes.

3. Stir in olives, vinegar, sugar, capers and oregano to eggplant mixture. Season with salt and pepper.

Eggplant Italiano

Cannelloni
with Tomato-Eggplant Sauce

Makes 4 servings

1 package (10 ounces) fresh spinach, stemmed
1 cup ricotta cheese
2 eggs *or* 4 egg whites, beaten
¼ cup grated Parmesan cheese
2 tablespoons finely chopped fresh parsley
½ teaspoon salt
8 manicotti shells, cooked and cooled
   Tomato-Eggplant Sauce (page 186)
1 cup (4 ounces) shredded mozzarella cheese

1. Preheat oven to 350°F.

2. Wash spinach; do not pat dry. Place spinach in large saucepan; cook, covered, over medium-high heat 3 to 5 minutes or until spinach is wilted. Cool slightly; drain. Chop finely.

3. Combine ricotta cheese, spinach, eggs, Parmesan cheese, parsley and salt in large bowl; mix well. Spoon mixture into manicotti shells; arrange in 13×9-inch baking dish. Spoon Tomato-Eggplant Sauce over manicotti; sprinkle with mozzarella cheese.

4. Bake, uncovered, 25 to 30 minutes or until hot and bubbly.

Cannelloni with Tomato-Eggplant Sauce

Vegetables & More

Tomato-Eggplant Sauce
Makes about 2½ cups

1 tablespoon olive oil
1 small eggplant, coarsely chopped
½ cup chopped onion
2 cloves garlic, minced
½ teaspoon dried tarragon
¼ teaspoon dried thyme
1 can (about 14 ounces) whole tomatoes, undrained, coarsely chopped
Salt
Black pepper

1. Heat oil in large skillet over medium heat. Add eggplant, onion, garlic, tarragon and thyme; cook and stir about 5 minutes or until vegetables are tender.

2. Stir in tomatoes with juice; bring to a boil. Reduce heat and simmer, uncovered, 3 to 4 minutes. Season with salt and pepper.

Note: Eggplant—the mainstay of Mediterranean cuisine—is prepared in more than fifty ways across the region. The purplish egg-shaped vegetable comes in a variety of shapes, colors and sizes. Look for an eggplant that is firm and heavy for its size, with a tight, glossy, deeply-colored skin.

Vegetables & More

Smoky Pan-Roasted Artichokes

Makes 4 servings

2 artichokes (8 ounces each)
3 tablespoons chopped bacon
¼ cup shallots, minced
¼ cup pine nuts
⅓ cup California Ripe Olives, wedged
1 tablespoon fresh parsley, chopped
½ teaspoon fresh thyme, chopped
2 teaspoons olive oil
½ cup chicken broth
1 tablespoon lemon juice
1 teaspoon Dijon mustard
¼ teaspoon salt
   Dash black pepper, coarsely ground

1. Remove stems and tops of leaves from artichokes. Cut into quarters and remove purple, fuzzy center. Place in steaming rack above pot of water; bring water to a boil. Steam 15 minutes. Remove artichokes from pot; drain well and set aside.

2. Heat a large skillet over medium heat. Add bacon, shallots and pine nuts; cook 2 to 3 minutes until bacon is crispy and pine nuts are golden. Use a slotted spoon to place bacon mix in a large bowl, discarding pan grease. Add California Ripe Olives, parsley and thyme; set aside.

3. Heat olive oil in large skillet over medium heat. Add artichokes; cook and stir 3 to 4 minutes until golden. Add chicken broth, lemon juice and mustard. Sprinkle with bacon mixture and salt and pepper. Heat and serve.

Favorite recipe from **California Olive Industry**

Grilled Asparagus and Peppers

Makes 5 to 6 servings

½ cup balsamic vinegar
¼ cup olive oil
1 tablespoon chopped onion
1 clove garlic, minced
½ teaspoon dried basil
½ teaspoon dried thyme
½ teaspoon lemon pepper seasoning
¼ teaspoon salt
1 pound thin asparagus, trimmed
1 large red bell pepper, cut into ½-inch-wide strips
1 large yellow bell pepper, cut into ½-inch-wide strips

1. Combine vinegar, oil, onion, garlic, basil, thyme, lemon pepper and salt in small bowl until blended. Place vinegar mixture, asparagus and bell peppers in large resealable food storage bag. Close bag securely, turning to coat. Marinate 30 minutes, turning after 15 minutes.

2. Prepare grill for direct cooking.

3. Drain asparagus and bell peppers; reserve marinade. Grill over medium-high heat 8 to 10 minutes or until tender, turning halfway through grilling time and brushing frequently with reserved marinade. Serve hot or at room temperature.

Grilled Asparagus and Peppers

Spanish Potatoes
Makes 8 servings (about 9 cups)

2½ pounds Idaho Potatoes, sliced into bite-sized pieces
1 (8-ounce) package sliced lean bacon
1 (10-ounce) package frozen diced sweet peppers
1 (15-ounce) can crushed tomatoes
2 cups water
½ cup chopped Spanish olives with pimiento
1 to 3 tablespoons chili powder
½ teaspoon onion powder
¼ teaspoon garlic powder
1 to 2 tablespoons chopped capers*

Additional capers can be used for garnish.

1. In large heavy skillet, cook bacon until well done and crisp. Remove from skillet. Drain on paper towel. Crumble and reserve.

2. Pour off drippings; add peppers to skillet. Cook 5 minutes or until liquid has evaporated.

3. Add potatoes, tomatoes, water, olives, chili powder, onion powder and garlic powder. Bring to a boil and cook uncovered, stirring occasionally, 20 minutes or until fork-tender. Stir in capers.

4. Let stand 5 minutes to allow liquids to absorb. Stir in crumbled bacon and serve.

Favorite recipe from **Idaho Potato Commission**

Spanish Potatoes

Ratatouille

Makes 4 (1½-cup) servings

¼ cup olive or vegetable oil
2 cups chopped onions
2 cloves garlic, minced
4 to 5 cups cubed eggplant (about 1 pound)
2 cups sliced mushrooms (about ⅓ pound)
1 can (about 14 ounces) diced tomatoes *or* 3 tomatoes, peeled, chopped
½ pound zucchini, cut lengthwise into halves and sliced (about 1¼ cups)
    or 1 package (10 ounces) frozen sliced zucchini
1 green bell pepper, cut into strips
1 teaspoon dried basil
1 teaspoon dried oregano
¼ teaspoon salt
  Black pepper

1. Heat oil in 5-quart Dutch oven over medium-high heat. Add onions and garlic; cook and stir until onions are soft. Stir in eggplant, mushrooms, tomatoes, zucchini, bell pepper, basil, oregano, salt and black pepper.

2. Bring to a boil over high heat. Reduce heat to low. Cover; simmer 20 to 25 minutes or until vegetables are fork-tender. Cook, uncovered, 5 to 10 minutes more until mixture is slightly thickened, stirring occasionally.

Romesco Sauce

Makes 5 (¼-cup) servings

2 teaspoons olive oil, divided
¼ cup finely chopped onion
5 cloves garlic, crushed
½ pound plum tomatoes, seeded, cut in half (about 4 plum tomatoes)
2 slices dry Italian or French bread, ¼ inch thick
¼ cup chicken broth
¼ cup pimiento
2 tablespoons white wine
½ teaspoon red pepper flakes
2 tablespoons sliced almonds
1 tablespoon red wine vinegar

1. Heat 1 teaspoon oil in medium saucepan over medium heat. Add onion and garlic; cook and stir 2 to 3 minutes or until onion is tender. Add tomatoes, bread, chicken broth, pimiento, wine and red pepper flakes; cover. Reduce heat to medium-low; cook 20 minutes or until tomatoes are very soft.

2. Place almonds in food processor or blender; process until a fine consistency. Add vinegar and remaining 1 teaspoon oil; blend thoroughly. Add tomato mixture to food processor or blender; process until smooth. Serve at room temperature.

Note: Romesco, a classic sauce from Spain, is made with tomatoes, red bell peppers, onion, garlic and olive oil. The mixture is ground with nuts, usually almonds, in a blender to thicken. This versatile sauce is served to enhance the flavor of grilled fish, poultry and vegetables.

Sweets

Cannoli Pastries

Makes 18 to 20 pastries

4 cups (32 ounces) ricotta cheese
1½ cups sifted powdered sugar
2 teaspoons ground cinnamon
¼ cup diced candied orange peel, minced
1 teaspoon grated lemon peel
18 to 20 unfilled cannoli shells*
  Additional powdered sugar
2 squares (1 ounce each) semisweet chocolate, finely chopped

Cannoli shells can be found at Italian bakeries and delis or in the ethnic food aisles at some supermarkets. If shells are unavailable, serve filling in dessert dish with sugar wafer or other cookie.

1. Beat ricotta cheese in large bowl with electric mixer at medium speed until smooth. Add 1½ cups powdered sugar and cinnamon; beat at high speed 3 minutes. Add candied orange peel and lemon peel to cheese mixture; mix well.

2. Spoon cheese filling into pastry bag fitted with large plain tip. Pipe about ¼ cup filling into each cannoli pastry shell.**

3. Roll pastries in additional powdered sugar to coat. Dip ends of pastries into chocolate. Arrange pastries on serving plate.

**Do not fill cannoli shells ahead of time or shells will become soggy.

Minted Pears with Gorgonzola

Makes 4 servings

    4 whole firm pears with stems, peeled
    2 cups Concord grape juice
    1 tablespoon honey
    1 tablespoon finely chopped fresh mint
    1 cinnamon stick
    ¼ teaspoon ground nutmeg
    ¼ cup Gorgonzola cheese, crumbled

1. Place pears in medium saucepan. Add grape juice, honey, mint, cinnamon stick and nutmeg. Bring to a boil over high heat. Cover; simmer 15 to 20 minutes, turning pears once to absorb juices evenly. Cook until pears can be easily pierced with fork. Remove pan from heat; cool. Remove pears with slotted spoon; set aside. Discard cinnamon stick.

2. Bring juice mixture to a boil; simmer 20 minutes. Pour over pears. Sprinkle Gorgonzola evenly around pears.

Pineapple-Orange Granita

Makes 7 servings

    2 cups pineapple-orange juice
    6 ounces diet ginger ale (¾ cup)
    ¼ cup white wine or white grape juice
    1 packet sugar substitute *or* 2 teaspoons sugar

1. Combine all ingredients in quart-size resealable food storage bag. Seal tightly; store in freezer until firm.

2. To serve, remove from freezer; let stand 15 minutes to soften slightly. Crush ice mixture with meat mallet. Spoon into wine goblets or dessert dishes. Store remaining ice mixture in freezer.

Minted Pear with Gorgonzola

Sweets

Nancy's Tiramisù
Makes 12 servings

  6 egg yolks
1¼ cups sugar
1½ cups mascarpone cheese
1¾ cups whipping cream, beaten to soft peaks
1¾ cups cold espresso or strong brewed coffee
  3 tablespoons brandy
  3 tablespoons grappa (optional)
  4 packages (3 ounces each) ladyfingers
  2 tablespoons unsweetened cocoa powder, divided

1. Beat egg yolks and sugar in small bowl with electric mixer at medium-high speed until pale yellow. Place in top of double boiler over boiling water. Reduce heat to low; cook, stirring constantly, 10 minutes. Combine yolk mixture and mascarpone cheese in large bowl; beat with electric mixer at low speed until well blended and fluffy. Fold in whipped cream. Set aside.

2. Combine espresso, brandy and grappa, if desired, in medium bowl. Dip 24 ladyfingers individually into espresso mixture and arrange side-by-side in single layer in 13×9-inch baking dish. (Dip ladyfingers into mixture quickly or they will absorb too much liquid and fall apart.)

3. Spread ladyfinger layer evenly with half of mascarpone mixture. Sift 1 tablespoon cocoa over mascarpone layer. Repeat with another layer of 24 ladyfingers dipped in espresso mixture. Cover with remaining mascarpone mixture. Sift remaining 1 tablespoon cocoa over top.

4. Refrigerate at least 4 hours, but preferably overnight, before serving. Cut into slices.

Substitution: If mascarpone cheese is unavailable, combine 1 package (8 ounces) softened cream cheese, ¼ cup sour cream and 2 tablespoons whipping cream in medium bowl. Beat 2 minutes with electric mixer on medium speed until light and fluffy.

Nancy's Tiramisù

Sweets

Panettone Cake with Almond Glaze and Mascarpone Cream

Makes 10 servings

Cake

½ cup pine nuts
½ cup golden raisins
½ cup currants
1 cup warm water, divided
1 package (about 18 ounces) lemon cake mix, plus ingredients
to prepare mix
1½ teaspoons anise seeds

Cream

1 cup ricotta cheese
½ cup mascarpone cheese
¼ cup granulated sugar

Glaze

⅔ cup powdered sugar
1 tablespoon milk
1 teaspoon almond or anise extract

1. Preheat oven to 325°F. Grease and flour 10-inch bundt pan; set aside.

2. Cook and stir pine nuts in small nonstick skillet over medium heat 4 minutes or until nuts are lightly browned. Transfer to plate; set aside. Place raisins and currants in 2 separate small bowls; add ½ cup warm water to each bowl. Let fruit soak 5 minutes. Drain raisins and currants.

3. Prepare cake according to package directions, reducing amount of water by half and adding anise seeds, pine nuts, raisins and currants. Pour batter into prepared pan.

continued on page 202

Panettone Cake with Almond Glaze and Mascarpone Cream

Panettone Cake with Almond Glaze and Mascarpone Cream, continued

4. Bake about 40 minutes or until toothpick inserted near center comes out clean. Cool in pan about 30 minutes. Invert onto wire rack; cool.

5. Meanwhile, beat ricotta, mascarpone and granulated sugar in medium bowl with electric mixer on low speed 1 minute or until light and fluffy. Cover and refrigerate.

6. Stir together powdered sugar, milk and almond extract in small bowl until smooth. Add more milk, ½ teaspoon at a time, until desired consistency. Place sheets of waxed paper under wire rack. Spoon glaze over cake; let glaze set 20 minutes. Serve cake slices with dollop of mascarpone cream.

Spanish Hot Chocolate
Makes 4 servings

3 ounces semisweet chocolate, finely chopped
½ cup sugar
Pinch salt
4 cups milk, divided
1 tablespoon cornstarch
1 teaspoon vanilla

1. Combine chocolate, sugar, salt and ¼ cup milk in large saucepan over medium heat. Cook and stir until chocolate melts. Combine cornstarch and ½ cup milk in small bowl; blend well. Set aside.

2. Whisk remaining 3 cups milk into chocolate mixture; heat until hot, stirring occasionally. Stir in cornstarch mixture. Bring to a boil; cook and stir 4 to 5 minutes or until chocolate thickens. Stir in vanilla. Serve with Spanish Churros (page 206).

Sangria Compote
Makes 8 servings

½ cup sugar
½ cup water
1 cinnamon stick
3 whole cloves
⅛ teaspoon ground nutmeg
2 (1-inch-wide) strips orange peel
2 (1-inch-wide) strips lemon peel
6 cups assorted fruits and berries: sliced, peeled fresh or unsweetened frozen
    peaches; pitted Bing cherries; blueberries; small, hulled strawberries; red
    and green seedless grapes; cantaloupe and honeydew melon balls;
    peeled, cored and diced pears
1 cup dry red wine or rose wine
¼ cup orange juice
1 teaspoon lemon juice
  Mint sprigs (optional)

1. Combine sugar, water, cinnamon stick, cloves, nutmeg, orange and
lemon peels in small saucepan. Cook, stirring occasionally, over medium
heat until sugar is dissolved. Cover; reduce heat. Simmer 5 minutes;
cool.

2. Place fruits and berries in large bowl. Pour sugar mixture through
strainer over fruit. Discard spices and peels. Add wine, orange juice and
lemon juice. Stir gently to mix. Cover; refrigerate 1 hour or up to 2 days
for flavors to blend.

3. To serve, spoon about ¾ cup fruit into each of 8 bowls. Pour about
¼ cup wine mixture over each serving. Garnish with mint.

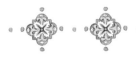

Polenta Apricot Pudding Cake

Makes 8 servings

¼ cup chopped dried apricots
2 cups orange juice
1 cup ricotta cheese
3 tablespoons honey
¾ cup sugar
½ cup all-purpose flour
½ cup cornmeal
¼ teaspoon grated nutmeg
¼ cup slivered almonds
   Powdered sugar (optional)

1. Preheat oven to 300°F. Spray 10-inch nonstick springform pan with nonstick cooking spray.

2. Soak apricots in ¼ cup water in small bowl 15 minutes. Drain; discard water. Pat apricots dry with paper towels; set aside.

3. Combine orange juice, ricotta cheese and honey in medium bowl. Beat with electric mixer at medium speed 5 minutes or until smooth. Combine sugar, flour, cornmeal and nutmeg in small bowl. Gradually add sugar mixture to orange juice mixture; blend well. Slowly stir in apricots.

4. Pour batter into prepared pan. Sprinkle with almonds. Bake 60 to 70 minutes or until center is firm and cake is golden brown. Garnish with powdered sugar. Serve warm.

Polenta Apricot Pudding Cake

Sweets

Spanish Churros

Makes about 3 dozen

 1 cup water
¼ cup (½ stick) butter
 6 tablespoons sugar, divided
¼ teaspoon salt
 1 cup all-purpose flour
 2 eggs
   Vegetable oil for frying
 1 teaspoon ground cinnamon

1. Place water, butter, 2 tablespoons sugar and salt in medium saucepan; bring to a boil over high heat. Remove from heat; add flour. Beat with spoon until dough forms ball and releases from side of pan. Vigorously beat in eggs, 1 at a time, until mixture is smooth. Spoon dough into pastry bag fitted with large star tip. Pipe 3×1-inch strips onto waxed paper-lined baking sheet. Freeze 20 minutes.

2. Pour oil into 10-inch skillet to ¾-inch depth. Heat oil to 375°F. Transfer frozen dough to hot oil with large spatula. Fry 4 or 5 churros at a time until deep golden brown, 3 to 4 minutes, turning once. Remove churros with slotted spoon to paper towels; drain.

3. Combine remaining 4 tablespoons sugar with cinnamon. Place in paper bag. Add warm churros, 1 at a time; close bag and shake until churros is coated with sugar mixture. Remove to wire rack. Repeat with remaining sugar mixture and churros; cool completely. Store tightly covered at room temperature or freeze up to 3 months.

Note: Churros and Spanish Hot Chocolate on page 202 are served in Spain as a great breakfast treat. The chocolate is thick and rich like pudding—perfect for dipping churros.

Spanish Churros

Sweets

Fig and Hazelnut Cake

Makes 12 servings

⅔ cup slivered blanched almonds (about 3 ounces), coarsely chopped
¾ cup hazelnuts (about 4 ounces) with skins removed, coarsely chopped
¾ cup whole dried figs (about 4 ounces), coarsely chopped
3 squares (1 ounce each) semisweet chocolate, finely chopped
⅓ cup diced candied orange peel
⅓ cup diced candied lemon peel
1¼ cups all-purpose flour
1¾ teaspoons baking powder
¾ teaspoon salt
3 eggs
½ cup sugar

1. Preheat oven to 300°F. Grease 8×4-inch loaf pan. Combine almonds, hazelnuts, figs, chocolate and candied orange and lemon peels in medium bowl; mix well. Combine flour, baking powder and salt in small bowl.

2. Beat eggs and sugar in large bowl with electric mixer at high speed 5 minutes or until mixture is thick and pale yellow. Gently fold nut mixture into egg mixture. Sift half of flour mixture over egg mixture; gently fold in. Repeat with remaining flour mixture.

3. Spread batter evenly into prepared pan. Bake 60 to 70 minutes or until top is golden brown and firm to the touch. Cool in pan on wire rack 5 minutes. Remove loaf from pan; cool completely on wire rack (at least 4 hours).

Fig and Hazelnut Cake

Sweets

Italian Ricotta Torte
Makes 8 to 10 servings

> 8 eggs, separated
> 1½ cups sugar, divided
> 1½ cups ground blanched almonds
> ⅔ cup all-purpose flour
> ⅔ cup HERSHEY'S Cocoa
> 1 teaspoon baking soda
> ½ teaspoon salt
> ½ cup water
> 2 teaspoons vanilla extract
> ½ teaspoon almond extract
> Ricotta Cherry Filling (page 212)
> Cocoa Whipped Cream (page 212)
> Candied cherries or sliced almonds (optional)

1. Heat oven to 375°F. Grease bottoms of two 9-inch round baking pans; line with wax paper. Grease wax paper lining leaving sides of pans ungreased.

2. Beat egg yolks in large bowl on medium speed of mixer 3 minutes. Gradually add 1 cup sugar, beating another 2 minutes. Stir together almonds, flour, cocoa, baking soda and salt; add alternately with water to egg yolk mixture, beating on low speed just until blended. Stir in vanilla and almond extract.

3. Beat egg whites in large bowl until foamy. Gradually add remaining ½ cup sugar, beating until stiff peaks form. Carefully fold chocolate mixture into beaten egg whites. Spread batter evenly in prepared pans.

4. Bake 20 to 22 minutes or until top springs back when touched lightly. Cool 10 minutes; remove from pans to wire racks. Cool completely.

continued on page 212

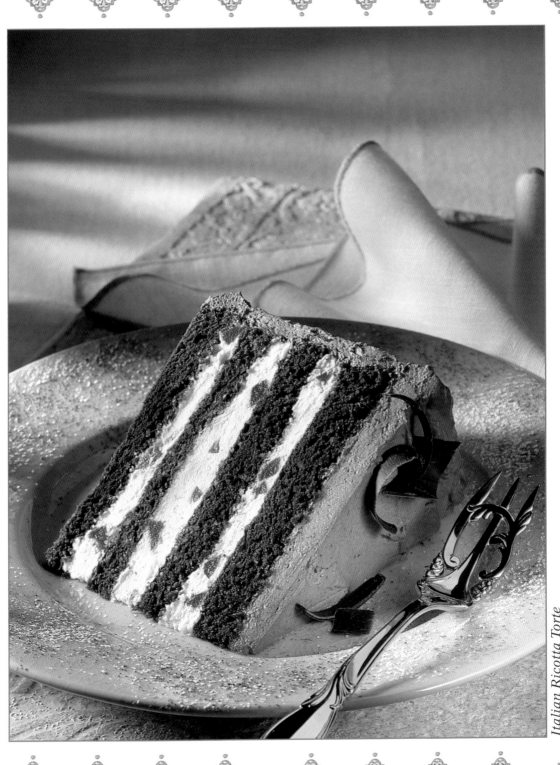

Italian Ricotta Torte

Sweets

Italian Ricotta Torte, continued

5. With long serrated knife, cut each layer in half horizontally to make 4 thin layers. Refrigerate layers while preparing filling and whipped cream.

6. Place one cake layer on serving plate; spread with ⅓ (about 1⅓ cups) Ricotta Cherry Filling. Top with another cake layer. Repeat with remaining filling and cake layers. Frost sides and top of torte with Cocoa Whipped Cream. Garnish with candied cherries or almonds, if desired. Refrigerate at least 4 hours. Cover and refrigerate leftover torte.

Prep Time: 40 minutes • *Bake Time:* 20 minutes • *Cool Time:* 1 hour
Chill Time: 4 hours

Cocoa Whipped Cream: Stir together ⅔ cup powdered sugar and ⅓ cup HERSHEY'S Cocoa in large bowl. Add 2 cups (1 pint) cold whipping cream and 2 teaspoons vanilla extract; beat just until stiff. (Do not overbeat.) Makes about 4 cups whipped cream.

Ricotta Cherry Filling
Makes about 4 cups

>   1 cup (½ pint) cold whipping cream
> 1¾ cups (15 ounces) ricotta cheese
>   ⅓ cup powdered sugar
>   ½ cup chopped candied cherries
>   ½ teaspoon almond extract

Beat whipping cream in small bowl until stiff. Beat ricotta cheese and powdered sugar in large bowl until smooth. Fold whipped cream into cheese mixture just until blended. Stir in candied cherries and almond extract.

Orange Almond Fig Cake
Makes 12 servings

10 dried figs
2½ cups plus 2 tablespoons all-purpose flour, divided
½ cup ground almonds
1½ teaspoons baking powder
½ teaspoon ground cinnamon
¼ teaspoon salt
1¼ cups sugar
½ cup FILIPPO BERIO® Olive Oil
2 large eggs
½ cup fresh orange juice
Finely grated peel of 1 orange
⅓ cup sliced almonds

Preheat oven to 350°F. Grease 10-inch tube pan with olive oil.

Remove stems from figs; cut figs into eighths. In small bowl, toss figs with 2 tablespoons flour.

In medium bowl, combine remaining 2½ cups flour, ground almonds, baking powder, cinnamon and salt.

In large bowl, beat sugar, olive oil and eggs with electric mixer at medium speed 2 to 3 minutes or until thick and creamy. Add flour mixture alternately with orange juice, mixing until blended. Add figs and orange peel; stir just until blended. Pour batter into prepared pan; sprinkle with sliced almonds.

Bake 50 to 60 minutes or until toothpick inserted near center comes out clean. Cool on wire rack 15 minutes. Remove from pan. Cool completely.

Sweets

Greek Lemon-Herb Cookies

Makes about 4 dozen cookies

2½ cups all-purpose flour
1 teaspoon baking soda
¼ teaspoon salt
1 cup (2 sticks) butter, softened
1¼ cups sugar, divided
2 egg yolks
4 teaspoons grated lemon peel, divided
½ teaspoon dried rosemary

1. Preheat oven to 375°F. Combine flour, baking soda and salt in small bowl.

2. Beat butter and 1 cup sugar in large bowl with electric mixer at medium speed until light and fluffy. Beat in egg yolks, 3 teaspoons lemon peel and rosemary. Gradually add flour mixture. Beat at low speed until well blended.

3. Combine remaining ¼ cup sugar and 1 teaspoon lemon peel in shallow bowl. Shape tablespoonfuls of dough into 1-inch balls; roll in sugar mixture to coat. Place balls 2 inches apart on ungreased cookie sheets. Press balls to ¼-inch thickness using flat bottom of drinking glass.

4. Bake 10 to 12 minutes or until edges are golden brown. Remove cookies to wire racks; cool completely.

5. Store tightly covered at room temperature or freeze up to 3 months.

Greek Lemon-Herb Cookies

Rice Pudding
Makes 6 to 8 servings

7 cups milk
½ cup sugar
2 cinnamon sticks
3 tablespoons butter
1½ cups short-grain rice
3 egg yolks
  Ground cinnamon
  Chopped toasted almonds

1. Combine milk, sugar and cinnamon sticks in medium saucepan over medium-high heat. Cook and stir until milk begins to simmer. Reduce heat to low.

2. Melt butter in large saucepan. Add rice; cook and stir 5 minutes or until rice is toasted and turns very pale golden in color. Add 3½ cups hot milk to rice. Cook over medium heat until milk is almost completely absorbed, stirring occasionally.

3. Remove and discard cinnamon sticks from remaining milk; stir into rice mixture. Cook and stir until all liquid is absorbed and rice is tender.

4. Whisk egg yolks in small bowl until blended. Stir ½ cup hot rice mixture into egg mixture; stir back into pan. Cook over low heat, stirring constantly 2 to 4 minutes.

5. Spoon into serving bowls. Sprinkle with cinnamon and almonds. Serve at room temperature or slightly chilled.

Note: Rice pudding is served in Portugal to celebrate major events. It is often topped with fancy designs stenciled with ground cinnamon.

Acknowledgments

The publisher would like to thank the companies
and organizations listed below for the use of their recipes
and photographs in this publication.

ACH Food Companies, Inc.
American Lamb Council
Australian Lamb
Birds Eye Foods
California Olive Industry
Del Monte Corporation
Filippo Berio® Olive Oil
The Golden Grain Company®
The Hershey Company
Hormel Foods, LLC
Idaho Potato Commission
McIlhenny Company (TABASCO® brand Pepper Sauce)
Mrs. Dash®
Mushroom Council
National Cattlemen's Beef Association
on Behalf of The Beef Checkoff
National Chicken Council / US Poultry & Egg Association
National Fisheries Institute
National Pork Board
Newman's Own, Inc.®
Perdue Farms Incorporated
Reckitt Benckiser Inc.
StarKist® Tuna
Unilever

Index

Index

Index

Index

Index

Metric Conversion Chart

VOLUME MEASUREMENTS (dry)

1/8 teaspoon = 0.5 mL
1/4 teaspoon = 1 mL
1/2 teaspoon = 2 mL
3/4 teaspoon = 4 mL
1 teaspoon = 5 mL
1 tablespoon = 15 mL
2 tablespoons = 30 mL
1/4 cup = 60 mL
1/3 cup = 75 mL
1/2 cup = 125 mL
2/3 cup = 150 mL
3/4 cup = 175 mL
1 cup = 250 mL
2 cups = 1 pint = 500 mL
3 cups = 750 mL
4 cups = 1 quart = 1 L

VOLUME MEASUREMENTS (fluid)

1 fluid ounce (2 tablespoons) = 30 mL
4 fluid ounces (1/2 cup) = 125 mL
8 fluid ounces (1 cup) = 250 mL
12 fluid ounces (1 1/2 cups) = 375 mL
16 fluid ounces (2 cups) = 500 mL

WEIGHTS (mass)

1/2 ounce = 15 g
1 ounce = 30 g
3 ounces = 90 g
4 ounces = 120 g
8 ounces = 225 g
10 ounces = 285 g
12 ounces = 360 g
16 ounces = 1 pound = 450 g

DIMENSIONS

1/16 inch = 2 mm
1/8 inch = 3 mm
1/4 inch = 6 mm
1/2 inch = 1.5 cm
3/4 inch = 2 cm
1 inch = 2.5 cm

OVEN TEMPERATURES

250°F = 120°C
275°F = 140°C
300°F = 150°C
325°F = 160°C
350°F = 180°C
375°F = 190°C
400°F = 200°C
425°F = 220°C
450°F = 230°C

BAKING PAN SIZES

Utensil	Size in Inches/Quarts	Metric Volume	Size in Centimeters
Baking or Cake Pan (square or rectangular)	8×8×2	2 L	20×20×5
	9×9×2	2.5 L	23×23×5
	12×8×2	3 L	30×20×5
	13×9×2	3.5 L	33×23×5
Loaf Pan	8×4×3	1.5 L	20×10×7
	9×5×3	2 L	23×13×7
Round Layer Cake Pan	8×1½	1.2 L	20×4
	9×1½	1.5 L	23×4
Pie Plate	8×1¼	750 mL	20×3
	9×1¼	1 L	23×3
Baking Dish or Casserole	1 quart	1 L	—
	1½ quart	1.5 L	—
	2 quart	2 L	—